THE STRONG FEMALE ATHLETE:

D1715729

A Female Athlete Guide To Reduce Injury, Improve Performance, And Increase Confidence

Dedicated To My Mom And Dad, For Giving Me The Gift Of Autonomy In My Soccer Career. Thank You For Being Loving And Supportive, And Not Helicopter Parents. I Turned Out Just Fine.

Table of Contents

FOREWARD

What comes to your mind, when you think about strength & conditioning and sports performance? For many, I am willing to say that it is high school football, the NFL, the NBA, etc. - all of which are male dominated sports. Too often when we talk about athletic development, we give examples of boys, and an overwhelming percent of the research is conducted in boys. In fact, a recent study (Cowley et al. "Invisible Sportswomen": The Sex Data Gap in Sport and Exercise Science Research in the Women in Sport and Physical Activity Journal) searched six journals and over 5,000 papers between 2014 and 2020. It found that a dismal 6% of sport & exercise science research included females only.

Hello… 1972 called – on a rotary dial phone! Have you not heard about Title IX? - a federal civil rights law passed in 1972 as part of the Education Amendments that protects people from discrimination based on sex in education programs or activities (including sports) that receive Federal financial assistance. Since the enactment of Title IX, there have been significant increases on a yearly basis in the number of female participants in sports, which at the upper end of performance has also created professional opportunities in some sports (WNBA, NWSL, LPGA, etc.). During the 2018-19 school year, the National Federation of State High School Associations estimated that there were approximately 3.4 million females who participated in high school sports. That is just the number of high school-aged females playing sports. This does not include millions of younger girls ages 5-13 years old who are participating and hopefully using sports as a major outlet for physical activity and fitness, and using it as a vehicle for many life lessons. Still, research and practitioner-led education remains filled with males; not only in the research and training methods, but also the researchers, practitioners, and presenters themselves are predominately males. There have been female pioneers in the fields of exercise science and strength and conditioning – for example, Dr. Barbara Drinkwater, Meg Stone and Andrea Hudy, to name a few, who have either focused on the female athlete or been educational role models for other females.

In this book, performance coach and consultant, Erica Suter, addresses several aspects of training and coaching young female athletes. I have gotten to know Erica over the past few years. Our first meeting was at the inaugural LTAD Playground in Philadelphia. Since then, we have shared several conversations on long-term athlete development (LTAD) and the youth female athlete. In fact, we also co-authored a blog – Girls, Growth, and Gainz – which several parts have found its way into this book as well.

There was a time when I tweeted - *Some of my favorite people to connect with professionally are those who possess a Master's Degree plus have a deep (not the same as years) practical experience, stay current, and understand the science.* Erica is one of these individuals. I have always been impressed with her years of experience and practical skills, often showcased on social media and her engaging with scholars on the academic literature. Perhaps more impressive is that she then turns around and implements the research into her daily practice with her youth female athletes – and then shares it with other coaches, parents and athletes. This provides an evidence-led approach to coaching and training the female athlete. In addition, she not only understands the "X's and O's" of training methodology for young female athletes, she also, and perhaps more importantly, understands the art and science of coaching, teaching, interacting and connecting with this population. This my friends, is why this book is a gem for anyone who trains, coaches, and develops young girls. It not only focuses on building the strong youth female athlete, but ultimately, the confident and resilient woman.

Joe Eisenmann, PhD

Chapter 1: Love for Movement

"If you don't love what you do, you won't do it with much conviction or passion."

– Mia Hamm

I stumbled into the house after dark. We had been participating in the usual shenanigans of childhood during the 1990s - drenched in sweat, rose colored cheeks, exhausted muscles, burning lungs. It took me a while to catch my breath after three hours of fighting with my brother and his friends. Okay, we were not fighting, but we were impersonating wrestling sensations, Stone Cold Steve Austin and The Undertaker. We imitated the pinning, the rolling, the escaping from a lock, and the body slams. Call this belligerent, but we were just elementary school kids being ridiculous, playful, and carefree. Mind you, we were unsupervised. In today's world, this all sounds foolish, almost dangerous, to the modern parent who wants to bubble wrap their girl from the uncertainty of the neighborhood environment and ensure she does not scrape a knee or get a boo-boo. Though our feet were dirty, and we were full of plenty of bruises and scratches, these years were the most defining of my life – the ages between 5-13 when all I did was leave the house for long days of physical adventure and movement. No parents allowed.

Wrestling was not the only activity we engaged in for a marathon of hours. We did Capture the Flag, tackle football, baseball, dodgeball, handball, kickball, Four Square, and Wall Ball. As the only girl in the group, I learned at a young age how to compete against stronger, faster, and bigger opponents. Losing these childhood games a plethora of times crushed every ounce of my soul, but I mustered up the competitive fire within me to beat the boys and come back with vengeance. I threw many crying fits, but the good news was, I found inside me the passion to compete and to battle my way to victory. I learned grit. I learned determination. I learned to challenge myself. I learned to fail. I learned to stand up for myself. I learned to use my muscles. **I discovered that my body was malleable to adapt to new environments, and capable of incredible feats of strength.** I easily figured out how to maneuver, how to run, how to stay balanced, how to shield, how to sprint, how to turn, how to twist, and how to be agile. While my body became strong, so did my brain. I became assertive, navigated disagreements, controlled aggressive impulses, and problem solved – all in the neighborhood with the boys. No amount of structured schooling and rehearsed trainings could have taught me these crucial life skills.

Movement was engrained in me during an optimal time in my youth - when my brain needed as much variety as possible for wiring new neural connections and making sense of the outside world. I had no clue that my brain was becoming sharper, and my athleticism was blossoming from the innocent play in the neighborhood. I developed the basic motor skills that were needed to further enhance my sport specific skills, such as balancing, falling, pulling, pushing, scrambling, climbing, grappling, throwing, aiming, jumping, and landing. These became my foundation and were the start of me becoming an unstoppable athlete.

Beyond the physical benefits of play, I developed the psychosocial skills to one day become successful as an entrepreneur, and fulfilled in my life purpose to inspire youth to love movement. I developed the independence to problem solve through adversity. I developed personal responsibility for my physical and mental health. I fell in love with movement early because it was a part of my lifestyle, and I saw it as fun, creative, spontaneous, and invigorating. Never was movement forced upon me, and never did I develop a bad taste in my mouth toward exercise. We were outside playing because we were filled with joy making up games, sprinting after one another, and roughhousing in the grass. In fact, my parents had to yell at us to come inside, whereas nowadays, parents **must cajole kids to go outside**. Had my parents forced me into a single, organized sport during the elementary school years, I am not so sure I would have a positive attitude toward movement. Had my parents not infused play into my childhood, I am not so sure I would have developed the autonomy to build my athleticism. Had my parents sheltered me from risk and outdoor adventure, I am not so sure I would have developed my mental resilience.

Fast forward to today, I am a college All-American athlete who still loves to move, strengthen my body, and is more motivated to work hard as my body continues to age. While many people worry about aging because of the inevitable musculoskeletal and cognitive decline, I get excited about it because I know how adaptable the human system is to overcome these processes. I know how movement creates malleability, builds new brain connections, and heals muscle tissue. **I know how movement keeps memory sharp, motivation strong, mood elevated, and life amplified.** Today, I feel in better shape, stronger, and more powerful than I was at the apex of my college career as a record-breaking goal scorer at Johns Hopkins University. In my eyes, movement is a lifelong sport, and I am thankful to still be playing it today with more passion than ever before.

I invite all young female athletes to start their journey of physical and mental strength, and be strong for a lifetime, even when they play their last competitive game. **Movement should not be an obligation, nor should it be a chore.** It must be a daily habit. I hope this book inspires the young female athlete to become strong and to shine with her strength in her mind, body and soul.

CHAPTER 2: The Early Specialization Debate

"Playing basketball had a significant impact on the way I play the game of soccer."

– Abby Wambach

I did not enter the travel soccer system until **age 13.**

For the female athlete of today, this is frowned upon, and results in being *judged* by her friends. Her parents are questioned by their neighbors, and she is forced into chasing the word "elite" as young as age 8. It could be everyone has a case of "keeping up with the Jones's" and lives in fear that a female athlete will fall behind if she does not do what everyone else is doing – more travel teams, more private lessons, more tournaments for a single sport. Of course, I am not passing judgement on parents nowadays, as I cannot say for certain how my mine would have acted in today's youth sport climate. I remain empathetic toward sports parents, and wholeheartedly feel for them, as they are put in a tough position on what to do with their female athletes.

Just like anyone else, my parents wanted the best for me when it came to soccer, but they drew a line in the sand and made sure it was still fun. Though travel teams sought me out all through elementary school, my mom did not give into the shiny bells and whistles, the higher status team, bragging rights, and parent peer pressure; and this gave me the choice to continue recreational soccer. She saw how much joy I got playing for a lower-level team, how many friends I made, how much I adored my coach, and did not want to disrupt my positive experience. This was a time when travel clubs were not as manipulative to parents with marketing tactics, alluring social media posts, and advertisements that shouted 'player development' as a guise for expensive year-round dues. In fact, club dues were minimal, and I remain thankful I grew up in a time when youth sports were not as business focused, but more so, human focused.

On top of clocking in thousands of hours playing with my brother and his friends, I was able to enjoy the exuberance of childhood. Since my rec soccer schedule was laid back, and I did not have to travel across state borders for games, I had time to sample sports like ballet, gymnastics, baseball, and lacrosse. I had time for being a kid. I had time to explore. I played in the front yard with my dad. We raked leaves and jumped into mountains of leaf piles for hours. My dad turned on the sprinkler and we jumped over the spray of the water. My dad chased us around the house as we screamed with laughter. My parents took us to the neighborhood pool. We did hundreds of repetitions of various jumps and flips off of the diving board. **Little did we know the sprinting, jumping, leaping, and playing built our feet muscles, body awareness, and reactivity, and would translate into better speed and agility in high school.** I knew no other side to youth, except for free play. There was no one barking at me to "run faster!" or have "quicker feet!" or to "play more aggressive!" All of these phrases coaches bark at kids are useless and do not elicit more effort on the athlete's end.

The fun games we played elicited the physiological response most performance gurus today promise, such as improved speed, agility and aggression. Better yet, we improved overall strength and built every muscle of our bodies through all of this movement variety. We stayed healthy and had no injuries, unlike many early specializing middle school girls who currently suffer from highly avoidable soft tissue injuries, such as stress fractures, muscles strains, and knee pain. The words "overuse," "burnout," and "ACL" were not in my vocabulary as a kid. In fact, I did not know what an ACL tear was until late into my high school years when a teammate of mine tore hers. To say I had an offbeat journey to what everyone is doing now, is an understatement.

How My Passion Began

My sports journey began when my mom signed me up for soccer at age 6. This was back in the 90s when there were no U8 "elite" teams, traveling out of state, and playing more games and having more trainings than professional athletes. Admittedly, I am nostalgic of these times when there were orange slices at halftime, 9 months of a true off season, and opportunities to sample a variety of sports without being benched by my soccer coach. Did I fall behind in this model? Was I too late to take one sport seriously? Did my soccer skills wane?

I did not join a serious travel team until age 13. Looking back, the recreational system was exactly what I needed to bolster my passion for the game. My rec coach was a volunteer dad who had a sharp understanding of soccer and who encouraged us to take risks. He never micromanaged. He never yelled from the sidelines. He never acted like every game was a U8 World Cup Final. We were just young girls who wanted to leave our practices and games with beaming smiles on our faces.

Because of the amazing coaches I had in the rec system, coupled with playing in the neighborhood and making my body incredibly strong from new environments, my physical capabilities soared – my balance, my coordination, my body awareness, my speed, my strength, my power and my agility. Because I was prepared physically, my technical and tactical abilities blossomed. Learning new soccer moves was easy because I had the foundation of coordination and rhythm to execute a skill with balance. Rocketing a powerful shot was easy because I had the leg strength. I did not need to be overcoached in my technical work. For my tactical ability, my brain was amazing at processing new information by the time I reached age 13, and I owe it all to the variety of unsupervised environments in which I had to navigate at a young age, without parents telling me where to go and how to react. In fact, I did not do a rehearsed "agility" drill until high school, and I am glad I never participated in the craziness of today where "agility" gurus put 8-year-olds through drills that look like synchronized tap dancing. Soccer is spontaneous and the play of my childhood prepared me for this. Also, it is a sport where not all work is done on the ball, as a large percentage of the game is played off the ball. Skill work is important, but it should never replace free play, as well as a well-rounded performance and injury reduction program. Many parents and coaches today still struggle to grasp this concept and fall into the trap that more focus on a single sport and specialized skill gets girls better at their sport, and will be more likely to become D1 commits and professionals. The messaging from clubs, such as "don't fall behind," "do our summer camps to get an edge," or the "10,000-hour rule" is a total disaster that preys on parents' and players' insecurities. It sends the wrong message, and makes parents believe that their girl taking off to enjoy neighborhood play, as well as strengthening her body will make her skills wither away.

This could not be more far from the truth, and both evidence-based and experience-based research supports this. According to the *National Strength and Conditioning Statement* on youth long-term development, exposing kids to a variety of basic motor skills, is the first step of the youth pathway to eventually boost sport specific skills in the high school years. Brain maturation is associated with neural plasticity during childhood and allows an opportunity to take advantage of motor skill learning (1). Unstructured play is one the best things a young female athlete can participate in for motor skill development, but also social and emotional development. It is sad because rough and tumble play is continuing to be demonized by sports organizations and educational institutions. Dodgeball, for example, is a game that is the first to be cut from physical education programs. Anxious parents and teachers see this type of game as violent, and that it must be controlled. Rough play like Dodgeball, wrestling, and grappling, encourages girls to navigate social situations as well as get comfortable with physical contact. Ever seen a young girl timid to go into a tackle against an opponent? Ever seen a young girl not playing aggressive enough? Ever seen a young girl unable to shield herself against opponents? Exposing her to grappling will help her to get used to this level of contact, and not shy away from situations with intense physicality. One of the greatest researchers on play, Dr. Stuart Brown, suggests that rough play allows kids to navigate their emotions, and is crucial for the development of social awareness, cooperation, and altruism. In his book *Play*, he expounds that lack of experience with rough-and-tumble play hampers the normal give-and-take necessary for social mastery, and has been linked to poor control of violent impulses later in life (2). One of the most fascinating and jarring studies done was Brown's research on serial killers. It showed that they had a childhood void of play and rough and tumble activities. All kids need this type of play because it enables them to take risks in a relatively safe environment, which fosters the acquisition of skills needed for communication, and boosts emotional intelligence (3). Taking the conversation back to early specialization, it pushes kids to participate in a repetitive, organized environment that is led by adults, instead of an autonomous and spontaneous one. We have enabled a society that is risk and play free at the expense of a child's physical, emotional and social development.

My good friend and colleague, Paudie Roche, who has worked at Arsenal as the Lead Academy Strength and Conditioning Coach for several years, feels the same. When I asked him, "what is the one thing youth athletes are missing?" he responded with, "free play." Please note that this is coming from a practioner who works in a system that cannot be anything but *specialized.* He is exposed to young athletes, who at the age of 16, sign professional contracts. Demonize specialization all you want, but their system is set up for them to train a single sport four to five times a week, with minimal time for exploring rugby, racquetball, basketball, and various other sports. Their primary sport is their full-time job.

Paudie continued to tell me that there is no escaping the specialized system, especially in Europe, and I would argue, now the United States. However, he said that the specialized athlete needs these non-negotiables: as much free play as possible, in addition to a quality speed, strength, and conditioning program. **I do not want to say I detest early specialization. Rather, I accept that it is a system that will be hard to undo, so there are a few options: remove the young female athlete from it, or maintain her carefree spirit and get her strong.**

Early Specialization and Injuries

A plethora of literature demonstrates the rise of injuries in an early specialization model, and the dangers it poses for female athletes who are going through dynamic changes during adolescence. The chance of suffering an overuse injury is higher for athletes who have specialized in a single sport, as opposed to those who participate in a variety of sports (4). A multicenter prospective clinical study that evaluated 1,200 young athletes (aged 7–18 years) showed specialized young athletes were spending greater amounts of time participating in organized sports while participating in less recreational activity. Specialized training resulted in an increased risk for overall injuries, as well as overuse injuries requiring at least 1 month recovery (4). For growing and maturing females, rapid changes in stature, strength, and limb lengths may heighten risk of injury when combined with intensive regimens of physical work (5). During the growth spurt, the female athlete body is extra precarious, and whoever thought scheduling four games in one weekend was a good idea, never studied the unique physiological needs of the growing girl. The female athlete body craves variety, so it can develop basic motor skills. It also craves rest, so her muscles don't fatigue. It also craves strength to protect her joints and bolster bone growth.

The push for early specialization might be well intentioned by adults, but it does not guarantee a successful and healthy female athlete. Despite glowing accomplishments at young ages, athletes who specialize at an earlier age experienced less athletic success as they became older (6). Girls are pushed to get in year-round repetitions of a single sport with the hopes of getting the scholarship or the national team selection, but the greatest players in history did **the opposite**. Mia Hamm, for example, played football with the boys. Alex Morgan was a multi-sport athlete who did not play travel soccer until age 14. Abby Wambach says playing youth basketball enhanced her jumping and tracking prowess as a professional soccer player: "Playing basketball had a significant impact on the way I play the game of soccer. I would go up and rebound the ball. So, learning the timing of your jump, learning the trajectory of the ball coming off the rim, all those things play a massive role." Adding on to these living, walking examples of exceptional female athletes, the UK Journal of Sports Medicine presented a fascinating study on the career of early samplers. Analysis of retrospective data across a multitude of sports from this study indicated that kids who participated in 3 sports or more between 11 and 15 years of age were more likely to play national compared with club standard sport between 16 and 18 years (7). To truly begin to help the next generation of female athletes raise the ceiling on their performance, as well as minimize injuries for their careers, it starts with escaping the robotic, specialized system and allowing them to enjoy childhood and build strong bodies.

The Importance of Play and Leisure

I get nostalgic of my childhood when play was my life – not organized sports, not adult-run activities, not specialized nonsense – just liberating, unsupervised play. Each movement was a step into novel territory, with new muscle groups firing. Each game was a plunge into new problems to solve, with greater cognitive development and my brain wiring connections. What exactly is play and why is it crucial for child development? Why is it paramount in the years 6-13 for female athletes to be immersed in play and not imprisoned by specialization? **The answer is simple: play is invigorating for the body, mind and soul.** Play is defined as an unexpected, spontaneous activity that is enthralling, yet relaxing. It can add a little anxiety, but in an exciting manner, out of anticipation of what is next. The anticipation is downright thrilling. Play can be the child jumping into a pile of leaves. It can be having a pillow fight with a sibling. It can be a dad tossing his daughter into the pool. It can be running in the dark searching for friends while playing Hide 'N Seek. It can be a thumb war or an arm wrestle. It can be a game of dodgeball. All these present uncertainties. They lead to belly laughs. They lead to nervousness. They lead to poise. They lead to thrill. They lead to problem solving. It is a rollercoaster that goes up and down with anticipation – the calm, then the exuberance. This is the "flow state" that psychologist Mihaly Csikszentmihalyi speaks of in his research. It is when someone is performing an activity and is fully immersed in a feeling of energized focus, full enjoyment and bliss in the process. The impact this state has on the brain is tremendous and plays a role in the development of the pre-frontal cortex and the connection of the left and right brain hemispheres. Dr. John J. Ratey, another researcher on youth exercise, presents several fascinating studies on how movement shapes the brain at a deeper level. In his book *Spark*, kids who exercised before class received higher test scores and better grades than those who were sedentary. The research does not stop there. Movement is also said to help alleviate ADHD, depression, and can be more effective than prescription medications like Prozac and Ritalin. This is because instead of drugs manipulating just one part of the brain, exercise balances all neurotransmitters – serotonin, norepinephrine, and dopamine (8). We want kids to love exercise and play, so they see it as a fun and potent medicine for a lifetime.

Movement is something kids are born with, so why would we stop encouraging them to move as they get older? After all, babies are the quintessence of the power of movement and how incredible the mind-body connection is to overcome new feats, like crawling for the first time, then rolling over, then standing up, then walking. The specialized system has disrupted the opportunity for play and burns girls out to even move at home. They are so gassed; they resort to plopping on the couch or scrolling their phones on their days off from obligations. They are so overscheduled with organized sports that the joy of free play has waned.

Amidst all the darkness, there is hope. It is going to take everyone getting clear on their values for their female athletes and taking radical personal responsibility.

Parents Can Change the Specialized System

➤ "We can do better for our children…"

➤ "The youth sports system is broken…"

➤ "It's become a business…"

➤ "My kid never gets a season off from their sport…"

I see the complaints splashed across my social media feeds. Parents are standing up to the nonsense. As fiery as the tweets are, these are not enough to elicit change. Though the intent is genuine and comes from a place of great care, the complaints are an unending abyss of all talk and no walk. Anyone can argue the system is broken, but who got us here? The evil producer that is youth female sports? Or the consumers who are the parents? As much as everyone wants to point fingers at the system, **it is the parents who are enabling it by swiping their credit cards year-round.** It is not like one day the $15 billion industry of youth sports is going to wake up and be like, "my bad…I won't take money anymore, let's just give several months off to young girls and let our money go down the drain." Nope. The youth sports industry will continue doing what it is doing because the consumer continues to pump money into it. Parents of female athletes are the consumers. So, what are they going to do about it?

Parent Peer Pressure

Peer pressure is not just exclusive to childhood. It permeates into adult life, sometimes tenfold, and goes without noticing. Adults are just as susceptible to the darkness of peer pressure, especially when reputation, status, and bragging rights are on the line. The industry knows exactly how to feed on parent insecurities and is clever with this in their marketing.

➤ "Don't let your kid fall behind…"

➤ "Get recruited…"

➤ "Get the scholarship…"

These taglines are captivating to parents who are living vicariously through their daughter. They are enticing to parents who want their daughter to do better than their neighbor's daughter. They are alluring to parents who want to make the college scholarship Facebook post. Many parents hate to admit it, but the peer pressure is real, very real. It is a bitter pill to swallow when they know they are pressured to do what is not always right for their daughter. Oh! That reminds me. The amount of money spent on club dues, skills lessons, and coaches like me is far more than what a girl will receive in scholarship money. Saying this would be a net zero is too nice, when realistically, it is negative money in the parents' pocket.

Once parents have a strong and deeper purpose for their daughter, they are much more excited, and not resentful about the investment in quality coaching, physical and mental development. There is a greater reason for young girls to play sports and train, and it is not monetary value, but rather, emotional value.

What's The End Goal?

- ➢ So, what is the end goal? Every parent should seriously ask this question.

- ➢ Do they want their daughter to be another ACL or burnout statistic?

- ➢ Do they want her to face nagging soft tissue injuries?

The youth sports industry rakes in billions of dollars, so it will not change until the consumer stops giving it money. Yes, that means the parents need to make sound decisions for their daughters. No more extra skills trainers. No more year-round organized sports. Imagine a world where a parent said to the head coach of his/her daughter's team:

"Here's what my daughter is going to do to improve her speed and be healthy for next season: she's not going to play for your summer team. She's not going to do your extra technical trainings. Rather, she's going to take off from going to your practices, and instead, play with her friends, work on movement patterns, revamp her nutrition to nourish her body, go on vacation to swim and surf, read her favorite book on Mia Hamm, and come back in the Fall strong and ready to play again during the season and make an impact on your team."

What coach would say no to this?

Alas, **if parents and young girls are scared to take a stand, then they need to understand that they are telling the industry to behave exactly the way it is and allowing coaches to push the year-round primary sport model, with no attention to the athlete's physical**

preparation. It is up to the parents (along with their daughters) to stand up without the fear of getting benched, bullied or shamed by a coach. It is up to everyone to set the boundaries, draw a line in the sand, and stick out like a sore thumb. It is up to everyone to hold coaches accountable. That is when true change happens for young female athletes.

As Arsenal's Paudie Roche mentioned, it is hard to escape the specialized system in the academy arena, but parents of the female athlete can pull their girl from practices, that indoor season, or that extra tournament. Parents can enroll their daughters in strength training. Parents can ensure there is free play happening in the backyard and neighborhood.

The specialized system might be here to stay, but it does not need to eat female athletes alive. Parents decide.

Sport Sampling: The Good and Bad

Sampling a variety of sports mitigates the overuse problem because female athletes are exposed to new movements that activate different muscle groups. A soccer player, for example, who plays softball in the off-season can give her upper body more love that she would not get in her primary sport. This helps her to build better posture and rotational power that translate to improved speed and agility for soccer. Expounding further, the best part is she does not overuse her lower extremity muscles (quadriceps and hip flexors) year-round and can still improve as an overall athlete. Some professionals would argue that sport sampling can include a single sport in addition to resistance training to give variety to a female athlete's regimen. The Pittsburgh Riverhounds

Academy performance coach, Mike Whiteman, makes a strong case that resistance training can count as a "secondary sport" because it exposes girls to new planes, new stances, new grips, and new fired muscles. I believe Coach Whiteman does fantastic work with his female athletes. I also support the notion to resistance train, but this setting is too structured, and does not give girls the benefits for brain development. **We must encourage both weight room preparation and free play to strengthen body and mind.** When female athletes experience multiple sports at a young age, as well as participate in unsupervised games, they are pushed to be aware of their bodies in space, respond to new stimuli, and learn new tactics. No weight room setting can give them the spontaneous decision-making that multiple sports provide. The truth is, both weight training and multiple sports need to be a part of a young female athlete's life. **Weight training allows her muscles, bones and ligaments to handle the high forces in sports, while multiple sports allow her brain to build from new environments.** For the parents who worry their young soccer player is slow to make decisions on the field, instead of enrolling her in rehearsed skills training, how about enrolling her in lacrosse or handball? These sports force her to keep her head up and on a swivel, constantly aware of her surroundings, which give her a more challenging stimulus than her primary sport. For coaches who are concerned their female athletes are tactically unaware of the field, how about having them play a fun and reactive game (dodgeball, handball, pinnie tag) in warmups with no coaching instruction? The female athlete brain is dying for not only variety, but also autonomy. Adults cannot give all the answers, and specialized training cannot be the norm if we want sharper, more aware, and more creative young athletes.

It's Not Always Rainbows

While I am an advocate for sport sampling, it becomes dangerous when done in the same season. Mind you, it depends on which sports are being played. A girl doing soccer and softball in the Spring will not do much harm since one is lower extremity dominant, while the other is upper extremity dominant. Nervous system overload does need to be considered, however, when looking at how hectic soccer and softball schedules are on top of academic load. Chronic stress could accumulate if a female athlete is jumping to soccer practice after school, then to a softball game, then scrambling to finish homework, then going to bed on overdrive. If sleep is impacted, then the stress is not worth it, as you will see in the coming chapters on sleep deprivation impact on injury risk.

The biggest catastrophe, however, is doing two sports in the same season that have similar physical actions, such as decelerating, cutting, and changing direction for a high volume of reps. This is too much load on the muscles and joints as these movements put the most amount of force on the body. Some examples include soccer with basketball, soccer with lacrosse, basketball with lacrosse, and field hockey with soccer. Doing these combos is a disaster, and sadly, the most common among female athletes today. I have seen it time and time again when a female athlete is juggling lacrosse and soccer, and they cry for help when they experience knee pain. Adding to the mess, if girls are not physically strong, their muscles are not equipped to handle the accumulation of change of direction, cutting and sprinting forces from these sports.

Personally, I learned this the hard way. When I was in 6th grade, I played lacrosse recreationally during the Summer when I had off from soccer, and it was the ideal set-up. However, as I got into high school, travel lacrosse clubs began to recruit me and ask me to play during the soccer season. Of course, I was bright eyed and allured by being a travel player for two sports, so I signed up without hesitation. During the Spring of my freshman year in high school, I was juggling both travel lacrosse and soccer, and while I thought I was invincible to the copious amounts of load, overuse injury crept in like it always does. And that is the thing: overuse is not as obvious as a fracture or ligament tear, but rather, something that sneaks in gradually, until it is too late. It starts as a minor pain, then amounts to an unbearable pain when a female athlete pushes through. During the season when I played lacrosse and soccer, rushed from one sport practice to the other, and played two to four games in a weekend, I suffered soft tissue damage in my IT band, as well as a stress fracture in my lumbar spine. When the pain began as a dull pain, I brushed it off and continued to plow through both sports, which is what many female athletes end up doing. Looking back, this was the worst decision I made, as my short-term gratification led to a long-term disaster: I was sidelined for six months healing both my soft tissue injury and my stress fracture.

Female athletes should steer far, far away from two similar sports in the same season because the load takes its toll on the muscles and joints, as well as the mind and soul. The stress accumulates when rushing from one practice to the other, while also managing school and friends. Overuse needs to be approached with great caution, and if a female athlete experiences even a meager amount of pain from the load, she should not keep playing. Remember, short-term gratification leads to long-term disaster. A female athlete's sports career is a marathon, so it is never worth it when she is young to push through pain (even minor) and put her future in jeopardy. It is worth it to take a season off, and to physically prepare for the violent demands of sport. Girls do not get a badge of honor for playing two organized sports in the same season.

Solution: *do the opposite of the system and your neighbors,* take a season off from primary sport to do another sport, play in the neighborhood as much as possible, and build physical strength with a performance coach. This goes especially for elementary and all middle school aged female athletes. For high school and college girls, this is when they begin to focus on primary sport, while also executing a year-round physical preparation program. Let us hope, however, they have an off-season longer than two weeks. If not, boundaries need to be drawn and the parent might have to pull the girl from practices to save her from too much load.

Physical Preparation Enhances Technical and Tactical

Taking the summer off from copious amounts of sport specific training to focus on physical preparation will not make a girl fall behind. In fact, quite the opposite. After playing recreational soccer, developing my movement efficiency for several years in childhood, and starting with a strength coach in middle school, at age 13, I had my first travel tryout. With my soccer ball scrunchie in and Umbro cleats laced up, I was ready to rock. There were 50 girls at the tryout, and truthfully, I was not too nervous. After years of stimulating my body with rough games in the neighborhood, competing against boys better than me, and learning how to load my body under the iron, I felt this tryout was my moment to shine.

I did more than shine, though. I dazzled. I won every 50-50 ball. I was faster than every girl on the field. I was two steps ahead tactically. I rocketed shots and scored goals. I was vocal and confident. What happened then? The coach of the top team offered me a spot within the first 30 minutes of the tryout. I accepted and began my high-level playing experience with passion.

Each year I fell in love with the game more and pushed myself hard in a relentless pursuit to improve in all areas of my game. I went on to play soccer at Johns Hopkins University, though I turned down several Division I offers from University of Wisconsin, George Washington University, and University of Maryland. At Johns Hopkins, I started all four years, was leading scorer every season (as a midfielder!), was MVP every season, was awarded Conference Player of the Year and National Midfielder of the Year, was team captain my senior year, broke the goal scoring record in school history, and was a two-time NSCAA All-American and Academic All-American. After college, I played in the WPSL against players like Tobin Heath, Leslie Osborne, and Heather O'Reilly.

I started travel soccer at age 13.

CHAPTER 3: Underprepared, Overtrained

"Courage, sacrifice, determination, commitment, toughness, heart, talent, guts. That's what little girls are made of; the heck with sugar and spice."

– Bethany Hamilton

Specialization did not enter my vocabulary until I began my coaching career. In 2012, I started as a skills trainer for young female soccer players because I saw a niche that needed attention. I wanted to help them get to a high level, develop confidence, and one day, enjoy the exuberance of college sports. Ultimately, I wanted girls to reach the apex of their careers when it mattered.

Though my intent was genuine as a rookie trainer who solely focused on the ball work, I learned quickly I was not giving girls what they needed. In fact, quite the opposite: I was part of the problem. It was a tough pill for me to swallow that I was enabling early specialization and causing more harm than good. I was making girls do endless skill work, having them use the same muscles repeatedly, and forcing them into overtraining rather than *preparation*. This revelation turned into a personal crisis because I reflected on my childhood and realized I was giving girls the opposite of how I developed as an athlete. Because of this, my clients suffered the consequences of my irresponsibility, and experienced injuries that 80-year-olds would have: IT band pain, knee pain, hip pain, and stress fractures. **This is where youth sports are today: female athletes are being overtrained and underprepared.**

The Non-Negotiable Path of Physical Preparation

I left the skills world faster than you can say 'overuse.'

My shift happened in 2013 when I began training in a performance environment and getting girls under the iron to build total body strength. I saw injuries decrease, confidence soar, and capacity to handle the game increase. Instead of hitting a wall, my girls entered high school with immense mental and physical strength, while their peers suffered from burnout, nagging overuse injuries, and ACL reconstructions. I sent my healthy, strong girls to Division I, Division II and Division III programs that suited them academically and athletically. Of course, I cannot take credit for their accomplishments as I merely showed them this offbeat path. They trusted me and executed everything I suggested.

Even today, I still get skepticism from parents who are peer pressured by their neighbors, who are suffering FOMO "fear of missing out", or who are enslaved by the "don't let your child fall behind" marketing schemes. Deep down, parents know what is good for their young girl, yet fail to execute what she needs. Anytime I have a new client come to me for training, 95% of them ask for skills training. There have been numerous times, even when I say no to tons of business, they still beg me to help their daughters work on sport specific work. If I do even an ounce of skill training now, I only teach them if they are really struggling. Furthermore, I urge them to practice consistently on their own time because most of the ball work can be done in the backyard.

The training girls do with me now is the most intense work that develops movement quality. It builds balance, coordination and spatial awareness, as well as total body strength, speed and power. I expect my female athletes to do the basics on their own, such as walking, skipping, crawling, balancing, and hanging from a bar daily. When they come to me, they can execute the max effort work like heavier lifts, sprints, and change of direction drills. **Repetitive skill work does not prepare them for the rigorous demands of their sports, nor does it prepare them for sustaining the most violent actions in the game. The equation is simple: when sport specific load is greater than muscle strength, that equals injury.** Lack of physical preparation leaves girls with weaker bones, joints, and muscles. Worse yet, they lack the cognitive ability – reactivity and field scanning and tracking - because they were not given new environments during the critical youth years of brain development, nor were they taken out of the same environment they get year-round from primary sport.

The skill work I was providing early in my career was not raising my female athletes' physical thresholds to perform and sustain max efforts during high level competition. Isn't this the point of training? To put the muscles and energy systems under greater stimuli than the game? The day of the game shouldn't be a struggle to survive. It should be the easiest thing a female athlete does because she is prepared physically. The preparation is hard, but a dedicated female athlete does it to handle every cut, every sprint, and every explosive effort. To be able do these movements repeatedly at max capacity until the final minutes of the game, without batting an eyelash, is the goal.

The ACL Epidemic

Thankfully, I have not had many athletes tear their ACL in over a decade of coaching. In fact, I have had only one girl suffer an ACL, but it was a side tackle that flipped her over with a high amount of force. This is one of those contact situations that is hard to avoid and is an incredibly unlucky aspect of the game. For non-contact ACL, these are much more preventable, and everyone involved in a female athlete's life needs to act – coaches, parents and youth organizations – to minimize these at all costs. As a matter of fact, one of the wildest stories I ever heard about a girl tearing her ACL was jogging during a warmup and taking a wrong step to only blow out her knee. What was even more jarring about this was, no one was around her. I heard this from a player of mine who was on this girls' team, and I was downright flabbergasted.

Excuse me, how the actual heck does this happen?

The answer is simple: lack of physical preparation.

A situation like this is catastrophic as much as it is idiotic. For a girl to blow a knee doing one of the least demanding activities (linear jogging) with no one around is a total disgrace. Mind you, she was on the nicest playing surface one can imagine: Bermuda grass. Along with other non-contact ACL injuries, this happens because of a lack of balance, coordination, awareness of one's body in space, and strength in the feet, calves, quadriceps, knee stabilizers, trunk, and upper body – all things that early specialization fails to address. I see girls come to train with me who cannot even balance on one leg for more than 10 seconds without wobbling. Meanwhile, clubs continue to add technical training nights, more skills training, more 3v3 tournaments, more showcases, more skills training. As the ACL numbers rise in an alarming manner, still, organizations are not providing physical preparation training. The results of a 2017 study showed that the ACL numbers rose drastically for kids, ages 6-18, with the rate of ACL reconstructions rising steadily by 3 percent for the last 20 years (1). U.S. Soccer even states that young girls are 4-8 times more likely to tear their ACL due to anatomical structure, muscle imbalances and lack of proper neuromuscular training (2). There are surgeons operating on girls ages 10-12 who claim they are sick of operating on girls this young. This should be heartbreaking as well as jolting for all, even for those who have not experienced it firsthand. Young girls are being overtrained, sleep deprived, less aware, malnourished, and not prepared, hydrated, fueled, warmed up, or strengthened.

The push for more of their sport continues to compound into muscle imbalances and compensations that manifest into injuries later in their careers. While the elementary school-aged female athletes seem all fine and dandy now, muscle imbalances are exposed the most in the high school and college years as sports get more intense and physical. The typical female athlete who does not have more going on than her sport year-round with minimal leisure, no resistance training, no outdoor play, and a crappy diet at home, with too much tech, social media and sleep deprivation will be the girl who suffers from:

> Over dominant quadriceps

- Forward head posture
- Unstable trunk and core
- Weak posterior chain (gluteal, hamstrings)
- Lack of coordination
- Lack of control of body momentum
- Inability to absorb force

The last one is the most critical because injuries are caused by an inability to absorb force. **If the muscles are weak, the forces go to the bones, joints and ligaments.** Adding on, if female athletes do not learn how to control their momentum and decelerate, they are much more like to tear a knee. In an ACL injury, compressive forces result primarily from inadequate absorption of ground reaction forces (3). The legs need to be strong, with the main muscle groups of the hamstring, quadricep, and gluteal muscles safeguarding the knee. However, the lumbo-pelvic region, which encompasses the muscles of the anterior core and low back, needs to be the most stable part of the body so the lower joints can also be stable. Poor core stability leads to increased knee valgus, and this contributes to increased ACL injury risk in young athletes (4). That said, core training should not be endless sit-ups. The stability of the trunk area depends on the stability and health of the spine, so when girls land from a jump or perform a cut, their lower extremity is much stronger to handle the forces. Anytime a girl's trunk sways too much away from the center of mass, this causes extra loading and torque on the knee joint. **Core training needs to be less sit-ups and more stabilization work.**

We also cannot ignore the muscle weakness impact on performance. If the muscles are weak, the girl's chances of being a faster, more explosive and more conditioned athlete wither, and she is not optimizing her potential. Remember, the most dynamic movements involve muscular horsepower to be able to execute with power and speed. Muscles are the fuel to the movement, and the engine to the car. Girls can never go wrong with getting strong.

The Brain's Role in ACL

I did not begin to see the brain's role in lower extremity injuries until after COVID-19 lockdowns in 2020. I noticed the girls who strength trained during this time, while also keeping a social, free play life with their friends flourished when they returned to play. On the other end, the girls who strength trained, but were not allowed out of their homes to be with friends, and who were trapped in anxiety and fear, were the ones who got hurt when they returned to sports. It left me scratching my head why they all had this in common. The mind-body connection is paramount to understand for reducing chance of injury in female athletes. If the brain is not trained to react quickly, then the muscles that safeguard the knee will be behind in their firing capabilities, thus increasing poor lower body kinematics. On the other hand, if the brain has not recovered enough and the nervous system is exhausted from fear or stress, then muscle compensations amplify, and muscles cannot fire to protect the joints.

More studies are coming out on this concept - the role of sensorimotor integration in lower extremity injuries amongst female athletes. Sensorimotor integration is defined as the ability to utilize sensory inputs from the external environment to shape motor output in the body. A girl needs to understand how to move her body in space when there are opponents around, decisions to make, and external stimuli to react to and maneuver around in a split second. The literature on the brain's role in ACL is compounding, too. Non-contact anterior cruciate ligament—injured athletes had significantly slower reaction times and performed worse on visual and verbal memory scores when compared with controls (5). Another study suggests that errors in judgment or inability to anticipate external stimuli may cause a momentary loss of situational awareness. If the brain's executive functioning is unable to negotiate the rapidly changing environment, reactive networks are disrupted. This causes a loss of neuromuscular control and inability to optimally regulate knee-joint stiffness to stability during deceleration (6). Another study that conducted a review of the ACL risk factor literature from 1951-2011 concluded that ACL-injured patients had significantly slower processing speed (7).

The research makes sense. The brain controls all movement actions in the body, so if it is not trained to handle the cognitive duress of competition, it will not be able to fire the muscle groups needed to perform high intensity movements. So how can girls optimize brain function to reduce the chance of an ACL injury? I can make a strong case for early sampling because other sports force girls into a new environment that the brain needs to adapt to and make sense of with new incoming information. The novel environment that is not their main sport, allows girls to tap into other neurological corners for decision making, and gets them exposed to new objects, motor skills, opponents, planes of motion, and body movements.

Take a soccer player venturing into the unknown and playing volleyball, for example. Instead of their head being down or level, they are forced to pick their eyes up for more repetitions to react to the volleyball. Frequently, coaches and parents nag their girls for being terrible with tactics and search for the solution that is primary sport (soccer in this case). The solution, however, is exploring new territory to get them to track objects, scan their space better, and pick their head up. For the primary soccer player, they can learn these skills in volleyball, tennis or lacrosse, and sports that encompass a high amount of hand-eye coordination.

Beyond playing a variety of sports, I can also make a potent case for non-traditional agility training to help girls boost brain function. I say "non-traditional" because this is where most coaches screw up. **Conventional agility drills are too rehearsed, not progressed enough, and are highly over-coached.** First things first: if an agility drill is being coached, it is not an agility drill. The only piece of agility that should be coached is the skill of change of direction – the deceleration, the re-positioning of the kinetic chain (feet to the shoulders), and then the re-acceleration. After this, every adult needs to exit stage right and stop telling their girls how to move. The nervous system is incredibly good at self-organizing, putting itself in an advantageous position, and it is smart with catching onto predictability. To that end, agility training for female athletes must make them fast movers and fast thinkers simultaneously. It must not be predictable. It is not setting up cones in various zig-zag patterns and blowing a whistle while barking orders. Girls need new environments that are more intense than the game. They also need adults to shut up so their brain can develop the blend of autonomous and rapid thinking.

Generalists Always Win

There is no question that female athletes need more variety and less specialization for their physical and mental output. While variety is a win for high performing and healthy athletic careers, it is also a strong augmenter to their pursuits outside of sports. The argument against the single sport, underprepared female athlete spills into how they function later in life in academics and careers. No lawyer ever specialized in just law. No doctor ever specialized in just medicine. No accountant ever specialized in just finance. These careers have more to them than their primary skills, such as being able to write emails, communicate with colleagues, listen effectively, speak in public, consult clients with empathy and openness, think critically and problem solve. A well-rounded human who is a generalist, with a sprinkle of a specialist will always thrive.

The surgeon who excels in the OR, but also has good bedside manner. The business owner who is strategic, but is also innovative. The teacher who is good at articulating material, but is also relatable and jovial. Generalization in coaching becomes paramount, too, as coaches need to observe the bigger picture of female athlete performance. One would think now that we are overwhelmed with more gurus, more experts, and more specialists, young girls would be better off – healthier, fitter, more nourished, more rested and less injured, but the ACL and overuse statistics presented earlier say otherwise. The specialists, whether it's the tactical coaches with no physical training knowledge, or the skills trainers with no injury prevention education, are adding to the mess of female athlete de-evolution. Youth female sports needs more generalists who see the bigger picture.

How Devolved Are Female Athletes?

Movement truly is medicine.

I learned proper performance training in middle school after my mom informed me about a summer speed and conditioning camp from one of my teammate's moms. My teammate, Sarah, was beginning to surpass our team in her speed and agility, and I saw her conditioning get to the next level. Never did she get tired in the second half. Never did her sprints slow in the final minutes of the game. Never did she lose a tackle. I remember being so impressed with her physical prowess, as the rest of the team plateaued. What was her secret? She was doing a five day a week physical development camp during the summer off-season.

Nowadays, the idea of this sounds as outlandish as solving Calculus equations upside-down. Even when I tell new clients they need to train a minimum of two times a week to elicit the best physical gains from my training, they drop their jaws and tell me how it will be tough to squeak into their schedule. **The moment any commitment is asked, is the moment people want nothing to do with this type of training.** Admittedly, I laugh at parents who say it is too much for their girl to strength train twice a week. During these conversations, I replay in my head the one-hour drive to train with my speed and strength coach…FIVE DAYS A WEEK back in middle school and all the way through high school.

Due to lack of physical preparation, youth female athletes have become motor neurologically immature, over trained, over specialized and under prepared. Throughout my coaching career, there were several girls who walked into my facility who could not skip with coordination and rhythm. It was shocking that they did not know how to perform a cartwheel. It was appalling to see them sprinting on their toes, and not using their arms while doing speed work. I remember lecturing so many parents on why we had to start with the basics because their kids' evaluations were dreadful. I remember girls rolling their eyes at the basics, wanting to jump straight to the advanced work. I always had to remind everyone of this: **youth female athlete development is a long-term pathway, and if a trainer does not hammer this home, then they just want a fast transaction as opposed to a *drastic transformation*.** The same applies in school: in order to graduate to algebra, one must be able to add, subtract, multiply and divide first. Physical training is no different, as there are gradual steps along the way to mastering efficient movement.

When I observe the social media world of performance, I see coaches with all the novel gadgets taking growing, maturing girls through resisted sprints and loading faulty movement patterns. Futhermore, girls who developed compensations from previous injury are still being pushed to the extreme, as their injury history is brushed under the rug and not addressed first. Even today, when I get a new girl who has even an ounce of pain or recent overuse injury, I do not assign her a full throttle program until she is completely pain free. But surprise, her parents want her to push for their instant gratification. Day in and day out, I reiterate to parents that their daughter's health is the number one priority. Running girls into the ground just for theatrics is ignorant, and good old-fashioned laziness on the coach's part.

Before pulling the trigger on an all-out performance plan and blasting it across the online space, have girls try these basic human tests (featured on my Blog at ericasuter.com) to see where they stand with their stability, strength, power and speed:

1. **Lunge Hold** – movement to showcase level of single leg strength, as well as any muscle imbalance or trunk instability.

Middle school girl standard – 60 seconds each leg

High school girl standard – 90 seconds each leg

2. **Max Crawl** – movement to showcase core stability, intermuscular coordination, and hip flexibility.

Middle school girl standard – 60 seconds

High school girl standard – 90 seconds

3. **Hang** – movement linked to mortality, and showcases shoulder strength, grip strength, and contributes to posture and spinal health. If girls can't climb across monkey bars with ease or hang for the time standards, it's a big problem.

Middle school girl standard – 60 seconds

High school girl standard – 90 seconds

4. BW SL Deadlift to failure

Middle school girl standard – 20 each leg without losing balance

High school girl standard – 50 each leg without losing balance

5. Pull-Up Hold

Middle school girl standard – 30 seconds

High school girl standard – 45 seconds

6. Broad Jump

Middle school girl standard – 5'5" – 6'

High school girl standard – 6'5" – 7'

7. 30-yard Sprint

Middle school girl standard – under 5 seconds

High school girl standard – under 4.5 seconds

8. 40-yard Sprint

Middle school girl standard – under 6 seconds

High school girl standard – under 5.5 seconds

So how did it go?

If They Failed

Congrats! The first step to knowing there is a problem is accepting the tremendous lack of physical preparation in female athletes. I will address proper physical training in the coming chapters, and why these movements are important for sports, so they will be on their way to being strong women on and off the field.

If They Passed

Boom. The physical journey does not stop here. It means more progression is needed in order to optimize speed, power, and strength. The good news is, they are ahead of the game, have solid muscular endurance, speed, and power, and have met the minimum requirements to physically train at a high level. Stay tuned for the next few chapters for proper loading and how to continue to progress.

CHAPTER 4: Growing Pains, OR Gains?

"Nature does not hurry, yet everything is accomplished."

— Lao Tzu

Before I dive into training programs, I must tackle the most ignored component of female athlete training: growth and maturation. Too often, adults ignore the multitude of physical and emotional changes during the female athlete growth spurt. This leads to frustration with their girls' performance and a lack of empathy with their oscillating emotions. The problem is, many coaches and parents think they need to be a pediatrician or medical doctor to be competent in this area. They do not, which is why I am going to simplify it, so everyone understands what is occurring during a female athlete's most critical years of growth.

What Is Growth?

Growth is defined as an increase in the size of the body and its parts. For youth female athletes, this can be an exciting time as much as it's a defeating time. For parents and coaches, it can be a time when everyone scratches their head as to why their daughter is tripping over herself in warmups, or slowing down all of a sudden, or on the other end, bolting past everyone during competition. The most paramount thing to keep in mind during girls' growth is this: every girl has her own schedule, so coaches and parents need to not only be forgiving about what is going on, but also act by focusing on the things she can control.

On average, girls begin their growth between the ages of 9-13, with the most rapid period of Peak Height Velocity (PHV) occurring, when girls reach a maximum height gain of 3 inches. This is when mom exclaims, "she shot up!" Parents can expect PHV around the age of 11.5. On the other end, there is the "late bloomer" who is left frustrated that she is not growing as rapidly as her peers. It may take her until 12.5-13 years of age to get there. She might become discouraged seeing her teammates out-sprinting, out-pushing, out-jumping, and out-running her. The growth spurt in young female athletes is not a time for adults to worry. Nor is it a time for them to berate their daughter for what is wrong with her, how her body is changing, and how she is performing. Rather, it is a time for coaches and parents to equip her with the tools to empower herself and focus on the things she can control to stay healthy, enjoy the sport, and be confident in her body. Put simply, no one should freak out, and instead, try to deeply understand growth and maturation.

Structural Changes

The funniest part about growth in young girls is that the most disoriented and perplexed people during this time are the parents, not the girls. It irks me when parents are angry at their daughter's lack in growth, which is so incredibly uncontrollable. Even when people say, "I just want my daughter to be toned or taller," I laugh. First, muscle is attached to bone so it cannot be lengthened by any means. Second, "toning" is a fancy word for "gaining muscle mass," which comes with training and age. Third, height cannot be controlled. The language adults use with young girls matters when it comes to getting in shape and experiencing growth (or lack thereof!), so utilizing phrases like "let us get you stronger" or "let us improve your performance" bode well without negatively attacking her physique.

The structural changes during growth are natural occurrences that cannot be altered, so rather, they need to be accepted. During the female growth spurt, the length of the bones grows rapidly, with bone mineral density filling in after PHV. The tendons and ligaments tend to be stronger than the epiphyseal growth plate, which can lead to fractures if load is not managed properly, or the female athlete is doing too much repetition of the same training. Hips widen which can increase the amount of rotational torque on the knee. As the tibia and femur lengthen, the quadricep muscle pulls on the patella tendon and this could cause a nagging pain or tightness in the kneecap area.

Weight Changes

The changes in weight can be the most offsetting for young girls, as several months after PHV they begin to gain weight in fat mass. Girls will have a low center of mass because this weight is distributed in the hips and legs. This is a natural process as the girl blossoms into a woman and prepares for birth one day. Breast development during adolescence is also what adds to the fat mass increase, so if a female athlete has gained weight on the scale, keep this in mind and understand it's a normal part of growth. This is called Peak Weight Velocity.

Dialing in on resistance training helps with body composition and improved performance. In females, Peak Weight Velocity comes after Peak Height Velocity (about 6 months later) and can be another frustrating time to add to the messy movement patterns. However, if they act on their resistance training, they can navigate this time much better and not experience movement awkwardness and performance decline. **Neural factors dominate a girl's growth spurt, and neuromuscular adaptations are improved by consistent performance training** (1). During the latter part of puberty is when muscle mass plateaus, and girls grow into their adult structure. Muscular strength gains are most prominent in female athletes when they reach the ages of 15-16.

Impact On Performance

These physical changes are important to understand how girls perform in sports, since the best predictors of performance during childhood and adolescence are age, size, body composition and maturity. The most notable impacts on performance are neurological disturbances. A wane in balance and intermuscular coordination (how the muscles function as one movement system) can permeate to declines in speed, change of direction and lower body power. During Peak Height Velocity and Peak Weight Velocity, girls may experience feeling "awkward" in their bodies. Consequently, they might be unable to control their momentum when changing direction, or they might slow down.

The good news is, decline in performance can be offset if girls focus on coordination, stability and speed training. As girls get older, surpass their growth spurt, and round out puberty at about 16 years of age, they have a muscular build that makes them faster, stronger and more explosive. These improved physical performance indicators align with increases in muscle mass, the "engine" that bolsters speed and power. However, girls cannot rely on muscle power to come naturally. While they will have a small degree of it as they get older, they still must optimize their muscular strength and power through consistent resistance training.

Emotional Changes

During adolescence, female athletes become more susceptible to oscillating and intense emotions as they develop their self-identity and place in the world. They are also starting to look outside themselves for affirmation, with the comparison trap creeping in. Young female adolescents spend a lot of their time comparing their physical capabilities to their peers. Although a lot of time is spent looking outside to their friends and teammates, family approval and support are the main guiding forces (2). It is critically important for adults to be aware of everything going on in their daughter's mind. When having conversations about the physical and performance changes happening, parents need to be cognizant not to use defeating language.

> Aren't these changes a big deal?
> Aren't young girls going through a lot physiologically and psychologically?
> Aren't these changes a lot for a girl to take on?
> Don't they need to have empowerment during this time?

The ability to take pride in accomplishments in sports can improve self-image. Showing girls their progress in physical training, such as improved stability, strength, speed and power is uplifting, and reminds her of how much her body and mind can accomplish. Encouragement is always powerful for a female athlete as she navigates physical and emotional changes. However, adults need to approach her with understanding and be cognizant to listen to her intently. The biggest mistake coaches and parents make with female athletes is not hearing them out and being quick to provide unsolicited advice. This is a big no-no when she is expressing her emotions.

As an example, if she is going through a tough time and is sidelined with an injury, coaches rush to give solutions. Instead of doing this, listen to her and allow her to do the talking. Here's a sample script to try:

Female Athlete: "This is so frustrating. I feel like I'm getting out of shape. I feel like I have such a long way to go."

Coach: *listen, take time to respond* allow her to keep expressing herself...

Female Athlete: "It's just so frustrating seeing everyone out there and being sidelined..."

Coach: I understand. Being injured is HARD. I know this is an especially tough time for you...

*you're repeating her emotions, showcasing you *listened**

Coach: Is there anything I can do to help or point you in direction to ensure you come back even better?

Female Athlete: Yes, I would love that.

A girl needs to express as well as process her emotions first before being attacked with logical, left-brain solutions. When she is in an emotional place, she needs time to work through them before she can think clearly and act. Approaching conversations like this with empathy also give her a safe and trusted space, and only bolsters her relationship with the adult figures in her life.

Menstruation

Oh! I forgot…there is more. To add to the physical and emotional chaos, the young female athlete must take on the most defining part of growing into a woman: getting her menstrual cycle. As a girl tries to find her place in the world, fit into her friend groups, and deal with her drastic body changes, her menstrual cycle just adds more for her to handle. While this can be overwhelming, coaches and parents can support and empower her to be at her best, physically and mentally, and dial in on her training, recovery and nutrition.

What Is the Menstrual Cycle?

The menstrual cycle is a monthly hormonal cycle that prepares the female body for pregnancy. The onset of a girl's cycle, "menarche," begins on average, at 12.5 years of age. While some girls begin their periods as young as age 8, there are girls who do not get theirs until age 15. Reasons for the various starts in menarche include genetic, nutrition, training load, and stress. If a girl is extremely early or late within this range, it is best to consult with a doctor to see if it is a unique case.

To break down this dynamic time, it is best to look at the four phases that occur during the span of 21-35 days:

➤ Phase 1 – Menstrual Phase

➤ Phase 2 – Follicular Phase

➤ Phase 3 – Ovulation Phase

➤ Phase 4 – Luteal Phase

If a girl is not pregnant, then the cycle repeats itself the following month. Understanding a normal pattern of the cycle gives insight into how healthy a female athlete is and if she is taking care of her body well enough. A regular cycle should be occurring monthly, and any time there is a missed period it can cause increased fatigue, decreased bone mineral density, increased muscle soreness, and decreased cognition. Missed periods can happen for a plethora of reasons such over-training, under-fueling, under-nourishing, and under-resting.

This is concerning for the growing middle school girl because it takes several years after her growth spurt for her bone mineral density to fully fill in. She must be fueling enough, getting adequate Vitamin D and Calcium, as well as resistance training to improve the durability of her bones. Stress fractures are one of the most common injuries amongst growing female athletes when they are not getting enough fuel and nutrients. We can easily prevent this with proactive conversations about missed periods and advise on how to tweak nutrition, so she is supporting her growth.

Hormonal Changes

Understanding the hormonal and physiological changes during each phase of the menstrual cycle helps coaches to structure a smart training program that keeps the female athlete healthy. Programming needs to reflect that of General Physical Preparation template, so girls are moving in an efficient way amidst hormone fluctuations during each phase.

Phase 1

Starting with the Menstrual (bleed) Phase, which is the official start of the cycle (Day 1), and bleeding can last 4-7 days.

There may be changes in mood, increased stress levels, and decreased neuromuscular control, due to the hormones progesterone and estrogen dropping during this time.

For most girls, this is when their energy levels can wane the most, and they feel the need to be introverts and close off. The girls may find their reaction is slowing down at practices, so coaches must be cognizant of the intensity of drills, prescribing more mechanics reinforcement (no new technical work), and moderate deceleration training.

In a study that consisted of 6812 active females, over 30% of respondents reported "stomach cramps" and "bloating/increased gas" during menstruation (3). These symptoms are of the most discomfort make female athletes feel sick and not wanting to train hard, and elite female athletes referenced that these gut symptoms associated with the menstrual cycle resulted in disrupted training and performance (4). Poor gut health causes a snowball effect of altered sleep and compromised immune function. There is growing evidence showing that a healthy digestive system plays an important role in the maturation of the immune system and protection against infections (5) and from an immunology perspective, compromise of the microbiome has been associated with allergic conditions such as asthma (6).

The good news is all of this can be alleviated by proper nutrition which will later be discussed in depth. Female athletes must nourish their bodies not just for injury prevention in the musculoskeletal system, but also, the immune, digestive and endocrine systems.

Phase 2

Moving on to the next phase, Follicular, which is when a girl blossoms out of her introverted ways and begins to regain energy. This is because estrogen rises again, progesterone remains low, and increases in muscle glycogen, fat, protein and water storage occur. There is also an increase in endurance during this phase, and it is best to work on aerobic capacity as well as low level, extensive plyometrics.

Phase 3

The third phase, Ovulation, is when the uterus releases the egg to prepare for potential pregnancy. The exact date of ovulation varies amongst girls, but for the average cycle it occurs on Day 14. Testosterone peaks during this time, and it can be an exhilarating time to reap the physiological benefits from more intense strength, power, and complex agility training. Energy begins to increase and peak, and girls might show up to practice with glowing confidence and sharp thinking.

Phase 4

The final phase, Luteal, is when hormones can get wild as girls begin to prepare for their next month's Menstrual Phase. Estrogen and progesterone peak, and there is an increase in muscle protein breakdown. Mood changes, irritability and fatigue come creeping back, as well as the potential of delayed reactivity in complex drills. The focus should be on recovery and stress management, and encouraging the girls to sleep extra (8-10 hours a night), and sprinkle meditation and calming activities into their regimen.

Stop Blaming PMS

Given the hormonal changes during the Luteal Phase, let us segue into the most well-known component of the cycle: Premenstrual Syndrome (PMS). Everyone knows about the dreaded PMS, the most aggravating time of a girl's period. However, this does not mean she should wave the surrender flag and succumb to its symptoms. It is a defeating approach to blame PMS and not act with easy lifestyle changes. Moreover, it teaches young girls to fall into a victim mindset, feeling like they cannot control their bodies and manage these harsh symptoms.

Newsflash: they can.

It is critical to encourage girls that they are in control and can take back their power within their bodies. The solution is not complaining, but rather, modifying their environment through daily habit changes, such as getting quality sleep, nourishment and recovery. The onus is on the coaches and parents to present actionable solutions to mitigate the most common symptoms:

- Fatigue
- Irritability
- Muscle Soreness
- Constipation
- Interrupted Sleep
- Cramping
- Bloating

Here is a list of what some girls might need to feel better during this time:

- Meditation
- Sleep
- Time away from social media and technology
- Nature
- Sunlight
- Walks
- Bigger breakfasts and more fuel
- More foods packed with B Vitamins, Iron and Zinc
- Hugs
- More hydration
- Naps
- Resistance training
- Alone/quiet time

Coaches and parents do not need to directly bring up the topic of the Menstrual Cycle; in fact, I strongly recommend against it. This is highly awkward and can make young girls uncomfortable. Instead, adults can be proactive with discussing these recovery techniques to their girls weekly for improved mood, energy, and focus.

Effect on Performance and Injury Risk

This is when the conversation surrounding the menstrual cycle gets complex. Several studies have suggested that the menstrual cycle does significantly impact female athletic performance, while others are not so clear. In a study done by Pallavi et al a difference during the follicular and luteal phases was reported when examining muscle function. They found that muscle contractions were more forceful and less fatigable during the follicular phase than during the luteal phase (7). Julian et al studied soccer players' performance in both an endurance test and a sprint test. Athletes' scores on the endurance test were significantly lower during the luteal phase than during the follicular phase (8). Sprint performance and high intensity running remains unclear in the literature, as there is no found difference in performance between the follicular and luteal phases (9).

As far as injury risk, there is no definitive research yet on increased joint laxity on increased non-contact ACL injury. Therefore, instead of making this defeating news our focal point, coaches need to shift the mindset to what girls can control as far as training and recovery habits. After all, the goal should be to lift young girls up and ensure they avoid the victim mentality. Since the training and recovery around the menstrual cycle is still a novel concept, it is hard to give universal solutions for all female athletes and give everyone an exact template to follow.

While more research still needs to be done in this area, here's what is known:

- Symptoms are individual and can impact performance (cognition) and recovery (sleep patterns)

- Symptoms can be alleviated through simple lifestyle changes as mentioned above (sleep, parasympathetic activities, and nutrition)

- Instead of changing training and delaying progress in a workout program, manage the symptoms first

Coaches can help by:

– Focusing on mechanics: fine motor skill reinforcement becomes even more paramount, from reinforcing landing mechanics to deceleration work, to change of direction technique

– Continuing to strengthen the total youth female athlete: when it comes to strength training, this can be an optimal time to reap the benefits of muscle building and help girls feel empowered and confident

– Focusing on recovering hard: coaches can be repetitive in their messaging to young girls and help them to dial in on nutrition, sleep and recovery lifestyle changes

Missed Periods and Common Injuries

It is urgent for girls to get in tune with their bodies and understand exactly when something feels off. Whether it is fatigue, chronic muscle soreness, disrupted sleep, loss of love for training, brain fog, or a missed period, these are all warning signs that something is not right. A missed period means a female athlete's hormones are out of equilibrium leaving her at a higher risk for:

➢ Low bone mineral density

➢ Musculoskeletal injuries

➢ Decreased immunity

➢ Decreased protein synthesis

➢ Decreased cardiovascular health

➢ Increased GI distress

Therefore, this book aims to provide every actionable solution for female athletes to stay healthy and keep their bodies balanced through proper training, nourishment, sleep, recovery and mindset.

Growing Gains: Keep Doing What Is Controllable

Given all of the significant changes happening during a girl's growth, this doesn't need to be a time of pains. Rather, it can be a time of **gains**. The greatest predictors of performance during puberty are age, size, and body composition, with body composition being the one thing girls can control so they can improve their speed, agility, and endurance. Gains in performance should be the focus for a growing female athlete because it gives her power back to control what she can. Introducing neuromuscular training and strength training programs are best during growth. The youth female athlete needs great care, but also inspiration to be her strongest, most athletic, most robust self. She will have the physical prowess to remain healthy and not be another ACL, stress fracture or overuse statistic due to negligence during training. As a powerful byproduct, she will also jumpstart her athletic performance.

Maturation

Maturation refers to how a girl grows into a woman, meaning how she progresses to a biologically mature state. Every coach has witnessed his/her team with varying heights, with some girls shooting up and some remaining short. Looking at a 12-year-old girls' team can be funky because a 12-year-old girl might be 12 chronologically, but over 13 years old biologically. On the other end, a 12-year-old could be 12 chronologically, but under 11 years old biologically.

Biological age can be determined by looking at height and physical stature (bone structure, build and muscles), and it is obvious who is maturing early and who is taking longer. For a more in-depth look into biological age and expectations for when a girl will reach full maturation, body dimensions and height, as well as bone age can be measured by the pediatrician. Admittedly, I am not a huge fan of taking a female athlete to a doctor to assess maturity status because the news can be deflating for some and cause more anxiety than needed. For example, when doctor diagnoses a late bloomer, they might say something like "she's maturing late" or "she's behind in growth" or "she's two years younger biologically" and this can cause a response that the young girl thinks "something is wrong with me." **My advice is: let her grow into her body as nature intends, ensure she finds joy in movement and her sport, and focus on sound performance training.** Visiting the doctor and getting the dreaded diagnoses is a waste of time and does more harm than good for the girl's psyche.

The Late Bloomer

The quote that kicked off this chapter, "nature doesn't hurry yet everything is accomplished" is a beautiful reminder that while things take their time to grow, they eventually blossom into beauty. Take a tulip, for example, when it is planted in a garden it needs 8-16 weeks of cooler temperatures before it sprouts to the surface. Once it is beyond the surface, it takes 15-30 days to emerge into its vibrant, lush bloom. What about a caterpillar's metamorphosis into a butterfly? I remember raising caterpillars as a kid and being so transfixed by the process. The fact that the process was a long one that required patience and care, made the emergence of the butterfly much more miraculous. Of course, I can give several more examples where nature is selfish, unwavering and slow with its processes, but the most notable one is child development. The growth of a girl, just like nature's magic, takes time. It is a beautiful process that cannot be sped up by man-made forces.

Recognize the Setbacks

When a girl is a late bloomer, she is behind 1-2 years in her physical development (biological age). Not only is the female athlete behind in her height and muscle, but her speed is also slower, due to a smaller stride length and less muscle horsepower than her early blooming peers. Oddly enough, this proves more frustrating for the coach and the parents. What's funny is that the girl is not always discouraged by her slow growth; in fact, sometimes she does not even notice it. But when the parent nags, complains, makes her short height the focus of the household, takes the girl to the doctor for a diagnosis, and hires all the fake speed trainers to rush the growth process, then the girl feels defeated, believes something is wrong with her, and feels she needs to run herself into the ground to catch up to her early maturing peers.

This needs to stop.

The first step when navigating the late bloomer process, is to move into the acceptance of nature because this is something that the girl cannot control, nor is it something she can speed up. It sucks, I know, but does constantly complaining and talking about how short she is help her to be better? Does it help her self-esteem if she is reminded about what she cannot control? Taking the conversation back to the emotional changes during this time, adding on to the storm of late bloomer drawbacks does not bode well for a girl's mental state. She already has the burden of the physical growth spurt disruptions to deal with, plus menstruation, plus hormonal and mood changes. So, for the late bloomer, it is best to encourage her to amplify her strengths (technical skills, agility, aggression and grit), and refine her athleticism with coordination, balance, stability, and mobility. When she grows into her adult stature, she can load with resistance and make tremendous strength, speed and power gains.

Good News for Late Bloomers

Time and time again, I have seen most late bloomers develop an insatiable desire to work hard and play aggressive against the big girls. Since they are not "handed" early physical advantages like the rest, they are pushed to play harder, get back up when knocked down, and dial in on their technical and physical training. When they get older, their mindset is equipped with the resiliency to handle anything, more so than the early bloomers who had it 'easy.'

Just like a flower, the late bloomer needs nurturing and time. We cannot yell at a flower to grow faster. We can only nurture her physical capabilities with smart and safe training. When a girl is young, it is good to remember that she should not peak in middle school. If she is the slowest at age 12, she can focus on what she can control (solid training) and allow the growth process to naturally unfold. As my dad told me, "It doesn't matter who is around now…it only matters who is around in the end." Wait until to the end, whether it is high school or college, when the late bloomer surpasses everyone else. Nature always comes around.

The Early Bloomer Considerations

Early bloomers will beat everyone. Stacked next to a late bloomer, they will outrun, outsprint, and outjump them every time due to height differences, and body composition differences. These female athletes have longer stride lengths, more muscle, more strength, more speed and more power.

While it is an exciting time to see these girls outlast their opponents physically, coaches and parents must not let them get arrogant or complacent. Too often, I have seen early blooming girls rely too much on their physical feats. They get lazy with their technical work, have clunky lower body mechanics, and have a first touch like an elephant, or trip over themselves when doing a one-versus-one move against a defender. Early bloomers still need to focus on their technical skills and not rely solely on their physical capabilities, otherwise the late bloomers catch up and are the ones surpassing the early bloomers in the high school years. This happens all the time – the early bloomers hit a wall, while the late bloomers have their time to shine.

Early bloomers also still need performance training, even though they have speed and strength nailed down at a young age. They need to learn how to control their momentum during change of direction movements, so their ankles and knees are durable. Once they built a strong foundation, when they are older, they can improve their speed even more, and do more advanced movements. A female athlete who took the time to build quality movement in the youth years will be much quicker to do the resisted sprints, the parachutes, the vertical jump mats, and all the cool exercises that involve a high amount of skill.

The takeaway message for the early bloomer: do not become complacent and keep building even if you are the best out there.

The takeaway for both the early and late bloomer: it is extremely hard to predict how good an athlete will be years into the future. If a girl is dominating at age 8, it does not necessarily mean she will dominate at age 16. To increase these chances, focus on all of the things that are controllable and that make a girl stronger.

CHAPTER 5: Building A Strong Female Athlete

"Training all comes down to anatomy and physics."

– Michael Boyle

Knowing all the disruptions during growth, the risks for injury, and the growing sports specialization amongst youth female athletes, it is time to get them strong so they can stay healthy. I am not talking about them surviving and getting away with the bare minimum. I am talking about them thriving and reaching their potential. **Here is what is expected: they need to resistance train.**

This should be a non-negotiable component for every youth female athlete team. It should be engrained in organizations and youth clubs as mandatory. Alas, it still isn't, and youth clubs, coaches, and parents see strength training as an option, rather than a requirement. The truth is, it is an absolute disgrace it is not required in a club system or in the household. To convince young girls to strength train means parents and coaches need to lead the way. They are the ones who know the alarming ACL statistics, yet do not act. Many still roll their eyes at hiring a strength coach or say they do not have time. This begs the question: do coaches and parents really want their female athletes healthy and performing at a high level? Are they ignoring the rise in ACLs? Are they just blaming it on girls because they're born females? Yes, the anatomical structure of females is different than boys, but the real issue underlying the ACL epidemic is the lack of priority with general physical preparation in female youth clubs and households. **More than the female sex factor, lack of resistance training is one of the biggest reasons ACLs are on the rise.**

The standard needs to be set from the top and it is time to take radical action. No amount of googling single-leg workouts on the web will save young girls. No amount of throwing together random balance movements is going to do it either. The ACL epidemic can be addressed by committing to a focus on movement quality and exercise progression with weights. There is no choice, as female sports are becoming more intense and competitive.

In today's world, youth female sports are like a UFC fight. The competition and stakes are high, and there's little room for error. Every girl is becoming more technically and tactically sharp, and now the most physically powerful girls not only stand out, but they stand out for longer because they've stayed healthy. The main reason many girls compete in youth sports is to play in college and eventually go to the pros. Parents push the scholarship route more and more, and girls are feeling the pressure. The chances to play at this level are lower than everyone is told, in fact, youth clubs are not fully transparent about what it takes to receive money and play at a university. Many parents are pressuring their girls to get a small piece to the "pie," but only 3.3% to 11.3% of high school athletes compete at the National Collegiate Athletic Association (NCAA) level. The number of scholarships given is also meager, so if a girl is not optimizing her performance and sustaining a healthy body during her high school years, it will prove tough to be seen in the crowd. Only 1% receive an athletic scholarship. In addition, only 0.03% to 0.5% of high school athletes make it to the professional level (1). It bears repeating that athletes who participate in a variety of sports during childhood have fewer injuries and play sports longer than those who specialize before puberty (2). To be seen, girls must be healthy first and foremost. To be seen again, they must stay healthy the next year. To finalize their college commitment and start their freshman year, they must stay healthy again. To enjoy the entirety of the college playing experience, they must...you guessed it...stay healthy.

There is no question that the female athlete needs to be built up at a young age and be given a strong physical foundation to build upon as she grows up.

What Strength Does for Girls

The benefits of strength training are endless, both for performance and long-term health:

➢ Improves body composition
➢ Improves knee stability
➢ Improves flexibility
➢ Improves bone mineral density
➢ Improves tissue quality
➢ Improves power
➢ Improves speed and agility

- ➤ Improves aerobic health
- ➤ Improves work capacity
- ➤ Improves mood

Improves mental health

Why not stay consistent with strength training? Young girls reap a tremendous amount of physical and mental benefits from getting under the iron. When they start young, they develop disciplined workout habits. Female athletes must commit to strength training year-round so they can witness their performance transform right before their eyes. **When they commit to consistency, they're allowed to progress faster and execute more advanced movements that build speed and power.** Building stability and strength are the foundation. Then the fun stuff can happen in the high school and college years. Consistency is key.

All female athletes need to be fast, agile and conditioned, but if they pop in and out of workouts with no real commitment, the progression will be much slower. First, they need to own the basic movements for at least several months. Some girls might need over a year or two, especially while they go through their most rapid periods of growth. As a girl grows older and begins to settle into her adult body, she can up the ante with loading movements to build hamstring, gluteal, anterior core, and quadricep strength. Movements like these should start out slowly, so girls can continue to own the positions and feel the muscles they're firing.

Likewise, they should be multi-planar to get girls out of the linear plane so they can reflect the multi-directional aspects of the sport. Dr.

Avery Faigenbaum, one of my favorite pioneers in research on youth resistance training has concluded in his studies that resistance training may support young athletes during complex movements, as well as help them to withstand the demands of long-term athletic competition (3).

To sprinkle in more variability, female athletes need to give their upper bodies love – the shoulders, back, and trunk area. Trunk stability is key for reducing the chance of an ACL injury in female athletes. If the core is unstable, it impacts lower body mechanics and ends up putting more load on the knee joint. In a study done on core stability, trunk displacement was greater in athletes with knee, ligament, and ACL injuries than in uninjured athletes, with lateral shifting of the trunk being a significant risk factor (4). When the trunk shifts laterally during a rapid cut or change of direction, this moves the knee into a more valgus (a "caving in") position, which increases the rotational forces on the ACL.

Even for sports that are lower extremity dominant, namely the quadriceps and hip flexors, building upper posterior strength becomes paramount so the body doesn't compensate with forward head posture, slouched shoulders, and you know, the typical slumped over posture of many female athletes. Enter: pull-ups. For those of you who have followed my work for a length of time, you know I have an affinity for pull-ups – paused, eccentric, towel grip and so many fun variations. There is not a single variation I have not tried because I love pull-ups and have seen the immense physical benefits – from helping my posture, to improving body composition, to making me feel like a strong woman, to improving my lower extremity lifts that require back and core strength (squats and deadlifts).

After young female athletes achieve their first pull-up, the mental confidence is huge. When they nail their first pull-up without any assistance, they realize how incredibly capable their body is of amazing feats of strength. I encourage all families with female athletes to have a pull-up bar in the household. In fact, the entire family can get on board with doing their pull-ups and inspiring a culture of strength at home. Hanging can also be done with a pull-up bar in sight, and I recommend the bar is placed in a common area, like the kitchen or living room door, so every time a girl walks by, she does her daily hanging and works on her pull-ups.

Strength Improves Body Composition

Body composition, which is the make-up of a girl in fat free mass (bones, muscles, ligaments) and fat mass, has a drastic impact on performance as well as the durability of the whole system. The bones, for example, need to be strong especially during the most rapid period of growth when bone mineral density takes longer to fill in. Resistance training improves bone mineral density, and ensures girls are not susceptible to stress fractures. German anatomist and surgeon, Julius Wolff, developed Wolff's Law which states that **your bones will adapt and become stronger based on the stress placed on them**. When you add load to the muscles, the bone cells, osteocytes, become stimulated and then regulate bone remodeling. This continuous loading has been suggested to boost bone formation (5). If not stimulated enough, the muscles surrounding the bone tissue can weaken. Therefore, resistance training and progressed plyometrics are highly recommended for young girls.

Building Acceleration

The most explosive movements in female sports – accelerating and sprinting – are the most exciting. Alas, many female athletes do not fill these buckets in their training. After watching many team practices, I saw most girls were not getting enough acceleration and speed work that focuses on clean mechanics and max effort work for time.

For acceleration, girls need to learn proper positioning of the shoulders and hips for optimal horizontal force production. There have been numerous occasions I evaluated girls on their 10-yard dash, and several of them would set up on the line with a slouched over posture, with their hands on their knees. Worse yet, their pelvises were externally rotated, and toes were not even facing forward. If they had to do a 10-yard dash with their best time, why were't they in a position to get forward quickly? This is because girls aren't taught how to produce horizontal force, and it is more reason as to why a performance program is paramount for female athletes to maximize these high output movements. Various wall drills, resisted accelerations, chest to ground starts, and hill sprints are some of the greatest tools for boosting acceleration. If coaches want to break down the form, the key cues are a split stance with a contralateral set up. This means, if the right leg is the forward leg, then the left arm is forward, so as female athletes accelerate, they are doing so in a coordinated manner. Other cues include: keep the hips low, shoulders forward over the knees, and back flat.

Maximizing Speed

Speed, also known as max velocity, is all about vertical force production, so upright posture, hip flexion (knee drive), and ball of foot strike are of utmost importance, especially with a malleable middle school girl who is learning speed and needs to get into proper positioning. Adding on, speed training needs to encompass drills that work on a rapid stretch shortening cycle for greater production of vertical forces, such as vertical jumps, depth jumps, and knee tuck jumps. Frequently, when I watch a speed training session for young girls, it encompasses these things:

➢ Ladder drills

➢ Sprints with minimal rest time (aka conditioning, not speed drills)

➢ Tapping feet in agility rings

While ladder drills and agility rings have their place and can be used as warm-up to build a foundation of coordination, and rhythm and body awareness, they are not the primary contributors of speed development in youth female athletes. It's always cute to see a self-proclaimed "speed coach" on social media posting kids running through obstacle courses and looking like dancers. Worse yet, he is not using any timing system to track data and improvement in speed times to the millisecond over several months and years.

When it comes to sound speed development, the goal is to create as much vertical force as possible with the fastest ground contact time. In order to get there, girls need to master these basics:

➤ Contralateral movement (opposite arm and leg)

➤ Ball of foot strike

➤ Fast ground contact time

➤ Arm control

➤ Stability of the trunk

According to testing done by Weyand et al, human runners reach faster top speeds not by repositioning their limbs more rapidly in the air, but by applying greater vertical forces into the ground (6). In the acceleration phase, they are creating horizontal forces, and as they reach top speed, they are producing vertical forces with faster ground contacts. Therefore, I discourage ladder and agility ring drills as speed training because athletes are not producing fast ground contacts and a high amount of vertical force. Too, these drills usually last longer than 6 seconds, which is a big no-no in speed energy system development. All speed drills must be less than 6 seconds in length, with appropriate rest between sprints of 60 seconds to 120 seconds or more.

Here are some speed drills to work on weekly and year-round to truly become faster:

1. Contralateral Movement

Why this is important: the more coordinated an athlete is, the more they can run with the proper gait patterning during top speed.

Expounding further, coordination is the foundation of having rhythm, which is also needed to be fast.

2. Ball of Foot Strike

Especially with female athletes, I see them striking the ground with their toes when they're performing skipping and marching drills. Additionally, they don't have mobility in the big toe when performing low level plyometrics. This prevents them from striking with the ball of their foot.

It is critical to make sure athletes understand how to make the ball of the foot bounce off the ground in every drill they do, so when they run at top speed, they are striking with the correct part of the foot. Stiff ground contact on the ball of the foot allows for greater production of vertical force. Too, the female athletes who "heel strike" need serious correction because they are placing large amounts of stress on the knees and hips, while also slowing down their stride rate.

3. Fast Ground Contact Time

Stop having athletes do plyometrics for minutes on end. Plyometrics are meant to work on shortening the phase between the concentric and eccentric muscle action, so ensure quality, fast contacts for explosiveness and speed.

4. Arm Control

While new research is still emerging on the impact of the arms at top speed, inefficient and awkward swaying of the arms across mid-line can impact the function of the lower extremity. Too often, I see many young girls swinging their arms across their body, causing their pelvic area to internally rotate and add torque to their knees.

Sprinting is lower body dominant, but according to a study in Strength and Conditioning Journal, "arms contributed 22% of the body's kinetic energy."(7) Arms are also used to keep balance during max velocity, and ensures that girls resist rotational forces and maintain enough vertical force in the ground. So, when oozing out a little extra from female athletes for increased speed, the arms can serve a great benefit in body control, as well as improved rhythm.

Arm mechanics can be improved by taking the legs out of the equation, then focusing on clean arm action in more challenging drills like marching, skipping, and galloping variations in new planes of motion. It takes years to master proper sprint mechanics, and it is even more difficult for female athletes who do not have track as their primary sport. Reinforcing the basics repeatedly through marching, skipping, knee drive, and arm drills is the best way to clean up form. Even the best track coaches say it takes the length of an athlete's career to master mechanics. All the parents of middle school girls who are frustrated with their girls' arm action or stride length can stop complaining and have their girls train consistently on mechanical work.

Sprint More

There is not a better stimulus for female athletes than sprinting. It gives them a potent combo of ground contact time, coordination, and vertical force production. In every female athlete physical program, it should be mandatory that girls sprint year-round, reaching over 40 yards distance to boost both acceleration "first step" and speed. One of my favorite speed experts, coach Lee Taft, speaks to the adaptability of the nervous system for speed development:

"Athletes have to be taught to go full speed so that their central nervous system adapts to the speeds in the limb control that they need. If younger kids are taught to move fast, and we gradually build in the technique, they are going to be okay.... When they get older, if they have had exposure to that speed, they can grow off that."

Early specialization has not helped with improving speed, either; it has destroyed it. What is ironic about this is, coaches are quick to recruit youth female athletes based on speed, or quick to cut the slowest girl from the squad. They love speed and see its value as they evaluate their team personnel, yet are quick to enable the specialized culture with minimal performance training programs that bolster max speed. First and foremost, there is little time for free play. By the time kids get done their four practices per week, their skills training sessions, school and homework, they are ready to plop on the couch and play video games or watch TV. If young girls would get out in the front yard and be chased by their dads, they would tick the speed development box for free and get ahead of their peers. Coaches, too, can implement speed at practices in the form of races. Performing drills that last under 5 seconds in length with a rest time of 120 seconds are the quickest fix to train speed.

Eventually, Speed Needs Consistent Detail

Girls must sprint as fast as possible a few times a week. If they are not getting this max velocity exposure in practices, they need to do it on their own. Then, the next step is to fine tune the details. When improving actual speed mechanics of the foot strike, knee drive, and arm action, this takes several months, if not years. A significant amount of time needs to be set aside to improve these crucial skills, and requires just as much time as time spent working on ball skills. Getting young girls in the proper positions is key, and this means slowing them down, so they understand how to strike the ground with the ball of the foot, or how to move the hands from eye socket to hip pocket, and not to cross the body when sprinting. This is not only great speed skill work, but also excellent aerobic work. It ticks the aerobic box to do continuous movement through marching and skipping variations, rather than do a mile-run that decreases speed and the intricate mechanics behind it.

Committing to early specialization has kept girls trapped in a technical drills and small-sided games box, with little exposure to sprint work. This becomes a cycle of "fitness" work with moderate intensity output and hasn't allowed young female athletes to raise their speed potential with max effort output. **Looking to team sports like soccer, basketball, lacrosse and field hockey, female athletes are rarely exposed to high-speed running.** They are tallying up more accelerations and decelerations – quick burst movements within 5-15 yards of space and not pushing past this threshold to achieve a maximum velocity effect. Playing a soccer game, for example, does not count as speed training. GPS data from U15, U16 and U17 female soccer teams competing in a national tournament tallied as little as 2 sprints to as high as 11 sprints (8). Another study done with female soccer players demonstrated that a training program of short burst and high-speed exercises improved linear sprint and agility performance in youth female soccer players more than small-sided games (9).

Young girls need to be exposed to max velocity to stimulate their nervous systems for fast sprinting, and this means doing so without the distraction of the ball. **The young female athlete nervous system is highly adaptable, so it is best to sprint one to two times a week year-round, whether it is through free play, formal sprint work, or a blend of both.** Girls need to also ensure they get appropriate rest time between sprints (over 1-2 minutes), so each rep is at max effort. If doing formal sprint work, investing in a timing system to track accurate data is a great way to see improvement over time, as well as elicit a competitive fire in the female athlete to get her to race against the clock. Personally, anytime I whip out my timing system, I see my female athletes run at their fastest, even quicker than a group race.

5. Stability of the Trunk

A stable core is not a ripped six pack. According to Serge Gracovetsky, author of *The Spinal Engine,* "the spine and its surrounding soft tissues has evolved from being the primary source of power to that of a controller of the power delivered by the hip extensors." The core musculature that surrounds the spine and supports it, enhances posture as well as allows for more controlled movement through the rest of the limbs during sprinting. Maintaining a stable core also means keeping the eye gaze up and looking ahead while sprinting so posture is not compromised.

Given that coaches have minimal time with athletes, it is paramount to incorporate speed drills that address the kinematics of speed development, build an athlete who moves efficiently, and develop them to have more strength and power. To summarize speed, the winning line-up for faster youth female athletes is this:

1. Sprint 1-2x a week (through free play, at practices, or in a formal performance plan)

2. Strength train 2x a week

3. Reinforce mechanical work year-round (march, skip, or gallop around the house)

It is that simple. No need for social media speed gurus.

Building Agility

Agility is the combination of being able to control deceleration, then perform a rapid re-acceleration in another direction. It is coupled with the cognitive component when a female athlete reacts to an external stimulus, such as the ball or a defender. I am not big on blowing my whistle and running girls through rehearsed agility drills. Instead, we do a lot of work on having crisp landings with jumping drills, and we focus on good eccentric control on both legs, single leg, linear, frontal, then rotational to get them in new environments.

A plethora of literature suggests that faster, more agile players produced significantly greater vertical braking and propulsion forces, and reduced braking and contact times. They also possess greater eccentric and isometric strength. Changing direction can be broken down into a rapid deceleration (eccentric, lengthening of muscles) to absorb force, then a rapid re-acceleration (contracting of the muscles) to produce force. In the strength and conditioning literature, it has been hypothesized that there is an association between eccentric strength, approach velocity and COD performance (10). Eccentric strength also allows faster athletes to complete the direction change with a shorter braking time, and allows a more rapid transition into a re-acceleration (11).

Taking the conversation back to the ACL literature, girls need to be taught how to react to unpredictable situations and build up their awareness in space. If there is any predictable drill I am going to conduct, it is done sub-maximally, and with the focus on getting them in Athletic Stance so they can re-position their ankles, hips and shoulders. Athletic Stance is the most advantageous stance for a female athlete's COD and agility because her center of mass is lowered, shoulders are centered, knees are slightly bent, and hips are low. This allows her to reposition her hips and shoulders abruptly. As an example, if a female athlete wants to perform a cutting motion to her left, that means her right foot, knee, hip, and shoulder should not be swaying too far to the right. These joint angles need to be in a more centered position for her to get left faster. Capping off a COD and agility session with fun games with various cues allows her to navigate an unpredictable environment like her sport. Cues that force her to keep her head up and scan transfers to the external stimuli she must react to come game time.

Frequency of Training

The truth: this all needs to be a year-round pursuit.

Even when seasons ramp up and everyone freaks out with overwhelming practice and game schedules, there still needs to be time for performance training. In-season workouts are low volume and meant to maintain strength. If these are brushed aside, do not be surprised when female athletes wither away and resort back to compensatory movement patterns, and muscle imbalances. The maximum time of detraining impact on a young athlete's strength is four weeks. They will not lose significant amounts of strength taking a four-week rest from a formal resistance training program (12). This does not mean sit still for these four weeks. They can still walk, crawl, hang, balance, skip, do light resistance training, and new set and rep schemes to recover, then get back into it again the next month. Because they did not stop moving and loading, they will be prepared to handle their pre-season with strength and resiliency. According to Tim Gabbett, expert and researcher on workload management, loading athletes to prepare for training and game load is a good thing. I remember I saw Tim speak at the Seattle Sounders Sport Science Conference in 2015, and he explained workload through a simple and hilarious analogy: drinking on your 21st birthday, and getting totally drunk and sick because up until this point, you never drank to prepare for this moment. Now, this isn't to support alcohol drinking before this period, but I love the analogy because it sheds light on how athletes need to prepare for an intense environment with proper preparation and resistance training, so competition is not more difficult than it should be. Everything comes back to the nervous system: when it is not prepared to handle stress, then come game time, the demanding movements will be a bomb to the entire system, causing fatigue and potentially injury. Loading, to that end, is needed.

Female sports are becoming more fast-paced, more physical, and more demanding that performance training needs to be a consistent habit and should not be secondary to skills training and practices. It is equally paramount and deserves a slot in the schedule to keep girls healthy. Mind you, performance training is one and the same as injury prevention training. The basics repeatedly compound into a better moving, neurologically adept, faster and stronger athlete. This goes for all levels, beginner and advanced alike, to revisit fundamental movements and execute year-round training with oscillating load.

I can't reiterate enough how important consistency is for female athletes. Everyone wants the overnight fix, or to make that fancy social media post. What people do not realize is that the female athlete in the social media post, who is executing more advanced movements, has put in years of hard work, motor skill learning, and progressive loading to get to this level. I once had a mom of a female athlete client send me flashy social media training drills to my email inbox nonstop. She would say, "my daughter needs to do this" and would micromanage my programming for her daughter. First and foremost, her daughter began training a meager one time a week and couldn't even do a basic deceleration or hip turn. Adding to the disaster, she was in-season and playing two games every weekend with three practices during the week. Doing what was on these social media posts would have been too much load for her and totally irresponsible on my end. Third, the most advanced drills that are seen on social media take several months of consistent twice a week training. The girl I was working with was not even close to progressing to these because her workout attendance was pathetic. After I told the mom that it took consistent twice a week training to get her daughter to advance to these movements and make progress, she left me as a client. Of course, I never take this personally because I know the magic of consistency and I am strong in my philosophy as a coach: **consistency is key for drastic performance enhancement.** Moreover, show up. Don't miss workouts. Be better than you were yesterday. Love the process. Don't expect the overnight fix. Nail these down, and you're guaranteed speed and strength improvements. As Leonel Messi said, "it took me 17 years and 114 days to become an overnight success."

Young girls can utilize this mindset for a lifetime, too. When they move into their careers, self-improvement stays with them and is needed to get ahead. Whether they go into accounting, law, medicine, investment banking, nursing, or academia, they will advance themselves and get promotions by continuing to do the work. Performance reviews in the workplace happen every six months to annually, so they better not have a complacent attitude.

A Word on Plyometrics

Plyometrics are not meant to make girls sore, nor are they meant to be done for hundreds and hundreds of reps. Too often, my young female athlete clients told me their coaches ran them through hour-long circuits of jumps, hops and bounds. To make this more catastrophic, girls are celebrating that they are doing phone app workout programs by influencers that have no rhyme or reason behind their programming. There is a cacophony of "thumps" and "thuds" as girls do box jumps or squat jumps or burpees for endless reps that tear their bodies down, and do not address the unique biomechanics of the female athlete. These drills also fail to address proper energy system development: the creatine phosphate system and the lactic acid system, the two systems that develop explosiveness. I know all girls long to become blistering fast. I know all girls hope to become powerful. I know all girls want durable muscles and tendons. I know all girls want strong bones. I know all girls want to handle the violent actions of the game. I know all girls want to sustain these actions and stay healthy. After all, team sports encompass rapid movements – goal scoring, sprinting, accelerating, counter attacking, juking, faking, cutting, diving, throwing, and jumping – that decide wins and losses, as well as fill the game with color and exuberance.

When we look at all these movements, they last no longer than six seconds (max 12 seconds), so why train these rapid, Central Nervous System heavy movements for longer than that? Why program "agility" drills that last 30 seconds in duration? Why program "plyometric" drills that turn into a 10-minute circuit with no breaks? Why program so much jumping, bounding, and hopping without nailing down movement competency first?

Is it to cause fatigue? Is it to make players sweat? Is it to give teenage girls more patella tendon problems? Is it to cause more overuse injury? Is it to fatigue their joints? I hope not.

Is it to tap into fast twitch muscle recruitment? Is it to develop power? Is it to build rate of force development? Is it to boost the health of the muscles, bones and tendons? Ah, yes, that is more like it.

Plyometrics are meant to build the female athlete up, so here are some pointers to keep in mind:

Master Technique

The adolescent female athlete is experiencing a myriad of physiological changes that continue until full maturation is reached – bone growth, menarche, coordination disturbances, decrease in balance, decrease in core stability and body control, and increase in fat mass. A study done by Araujo suggests that trunk dominant core stability training improves landing kinetics and may reduce lower extremity injury risk in female athletes (13). More studies show that core stability provides distal mobility, spinal stability and proximal stability (14), so we must keep the importance of the effect on lower body kinematics when more forces are applied to the muscles and tendons. With the growing female athlete, patellar pain in the knee runs rampant, so we want to avoid high forces placed on top of bad form – falling forward, core collapsing, weight on the toes. Instead, maintaining posture and stable core, and pushing the weight through the ball of the foot should be addressed. It is imperative to learn trunk control first, before aiming for the stars with jump height and tons of sets and reps without control over the landings.

With so many dynamic changes occurring in the body, female athletes must master plyometric technique and learn to pump the brakes and build a foundation for tendons to handle high forces. As a starting point, ensuring girls learn Athletic Stance first allows them to get into a position where they recruit all the muscles involved in absorbing force –

the quadriceps, the glutes, the hamstrings, and the anterior core all working together simultaneously. Once they nail this down, they can work on handling eccentric muscle actions from the landing. To quote track coach Tony Holler, "whatever force you can absorb, you can generate."

Moving to single leg plyometrics is the same game: get comfy with the eccentric component first. In fact, when single leg plyometrics are prescribed for youth female athletes, have them hold their landings for at least 5 seconds so they can truly feel the movement, keep their balance and foot flat, and know what muscles they are firing. And then guess what? Add in the concentric component.

The mastery of technique with plyometrics also requires teaching athletes' *spatial awareness* – the control of their limbs in space during movement. Are they in control of their posture when landing, or are they falling forward? Are they loading their knee joint too much, or are they falling backward, and unable to recruit the glutes, hamstrings and quadriceps? Are they able to maintain an athletic position? Are they able to push through the mid-foot? Are they able to keep posture from collapsing? Are they able to progress from linear to lateral to rotational plyometrics? If so, they can progress from vertical double-leg jumps to vertical single-leg jumps, lateral double-leg jumps, lateral single-leg jumps, and transverse jumps.

I would be remiss not to mention plyometric training is *neuromuscular training,* not hypertrophy or strength training. The nervous system is the prime driver in *elasticity* and the ability to quickly go from eccentric to concentric action (jump, land, explode back up). We do not want fatigue…we want swift movements! Quick duration, long rest. Then go FAST again.

Produce More Force.

After hammering down technique, it is time for female athletes to produce force. After all, the intent of plyometrics is muscle recruitment (fast twitch), muscle coordination, and ground reaction force. One way to do this is to ensure athletes have a rapid bounce in their jumps. I like to cue with snapping my fingers rapidly, so they keep up with the speed from an auditory cue. Another external cue that has worked magic has been the word "bounce." There is something that sticks with young female athletes when you tell them to be bouncy in their hops like a pogo stick.

As far as assessment, for vertical jumps, an excellent score for adolescents is > 20-24 inches.

Progress with Load and Vector Angles.

I know we all want the cool jumps we see splashed on social media. But did we get the form down? Okay, good.

There are several ways to progress plyometrics.

> ➢ Add volume in preparatory phase (jumping rope is excellent for elementary and middle schoolers)
> ➢ Decrease volume, increase intensity
> ➢ Perform in lateral or rotational plane

➤ Perform single leg

➤ Add load or depth

Keep in mind that when you add load, the reps must still be rapid. If they are not, especially after coaching cues, the load is too heavy.

Be meticulous with work-to-rest times.

I am going to get straight to the point here: keep the nervous system in mind. Plyometrics will tax it the most, so chill out and rest between sets so each set can be full force. Do not try to be hero who does long duration plyometrics and tries to squeak out every ounce of force production under fatigue. Ideally, a 1:10 or 1:12 work-rest ratio is best, depending on the work you opt for. A depth jump has a greater eccentric demand, so a longer rest time bodes well (1:12). A mini vertical jump series may call for a shorter rest time (1:10).

A strong female athlete works on the entire spectrum of performance training with strength, power, speed and agility work.

Load Monitoring and When Injuries Happen

As long as a female athlete is doing year-round performance training, she stands a fighting chance to stay healthy amidst a heavily scheduled, specialized system. Another component of performance coaches and parents need to pay attention to is *load monitoring*. I do not want to make this topic complex, so here is what you need to know:

1. Two games in one weekend are a disaster.

2. Two high school games in one week is another disaster.

3. In order to fully recover the muscle damage and oxidative stress from a match, athletes need a 48-72-hour recovery window.

4. This means, the high school schedule of Mon/Wed or Tues/Thurs games is a train wreck.

Let me keep it simple: playing minutes will need to be tweaked if game schedules are this crammed, and recovery (sleep and nutrition) will need to be optimized even more. Even for the strong female athlete who does her performance training, the templates listed above only exacerbate injury risk. I've seen parents pull their girls from that second game. I've seen incredible coaches play the non-starters to give the starters a rest that second game. Adults need to be smart and meticulous, and allow for the 48–72-hour recovery window to do its job, and not break down the female athlete even more.

With that said, there are many negligent coaches out there, and given female sports are fast paced, physically demanding, and aggressive, injuries are most likely inevitable. It is hard for a female athlete to go through her full athletic career unscathed. In all my years of coaching, when even the smallest injury happens, everyone freaks out. We have grown into a culture that tries to avoid pain at all costs, and this is not meant to sound unempathetic, but it is meant to let everyone know pain is a natural part of the healing process. Even the strongest and most conditioned young female athletes can get hurt due to the intense nature of sports and the crowded game schedules, but they might be lucky to have a minor injury rather than a major one because their bodies were prepared through year-round training.

Even though I was one of the strongest girls in high school, I still suffered from fluke injuries like ankle sprains, a hand fracture, and IT band soreness. The IT band injury, however, was from playing lacrosse and soccer during the same season, which I did not know was a big no-no back then. Again, I strongly advise young female athletes to avoid playing multiple, organized sports in the same season. As I dealt with minor setbacks, I saw other girls getting far worse injuries and even surgeries, and guess what? These were the girls who refused to learn weightlifting in the off-season. To that end, some girls will suffer more serious injuries than others, and some will get minor ones such as low-grade ankle sprains, soft tissue injuries, hairline fractures, or bone bruises. When any injury happens, this does not mean a female athlete should rest and couch surf for the length of her recovery. **Even when an injury is more severe, training can still be done around the injury.**

A common scenario is a girl who gets hurt and her parents take her to the doctor immediately. The doctor gives the magical diagnosis and speaks in medical jargon. The parents then do everything the doctor suggests, which is the usual, "just rest for a couple weeks." This is dangerous for a couple of reasons. First, doctors treat the symptoms, not the cause. For example, if a female athlete sprains her ankle, the doctor might attribute the injury to a weak ankle. However, what if the ankle rolled because of a weakness in the Gluteus Medius? What if the girl's core was not stable enough to control her lower extremity? What if the girl has not even trained her muscular endurance to be able to balance on one leg for more than a minute? What if the girl did not fuel with enough carbohydrates, and her muscles fatigued in the second half, causing fault to the lower mechanics? There is always more to the story than the injured joint being at fault, and it being an acute problem. Second, the parents and girl take the doctor's advice of "rest for a couple weeks" as "do not move anything." At least, this is what people assume the doctor means – to take off from all activity and chill on the sofa.

My advice: do the opposite of what the doctor says. **The truth is, the body heals through movement, the body continues to stay strong through movement, and the body avoids deconditioning through movement.** If a girl sprains her ankle and lies defeated in her bed for her entire recovery, her muscles have not only waned in the injured area, but also the uninjured areas. Sure, her ankle may be out of commission, but she has three other limbs and a trunk to keep stimulating so she comes back stronger. The injured area also needs to be moved so blood flow can get to the area, remove waste, and decrease inflammation. Even if it means moving the ankle a few millimeters, it is facilitating the healing process.

Injured female athletes believe they do not have to work hard, but I would argue they must work way harder than their healthy teammates. A girl should eventually be in beast mode and be a resilient athlete post injury, so she better be ready to put in the work. An athlete of mine who suffered the contact ACL fluke was totally defeated the first few weeks, but then took her rehab seriously and trained harder than her teammates. She was crushing Pull-Ups, Push-Ups, Singe Leg RDLs, and quickly gaining range of motion back in her knee just a month after surgery. She worked closely with her physical therapist and me in a collaborative effort to get her back to better condition than she was prior to injury.

Beyond her physical training, she took her mental training to the next level. When she was not working with her physical therapist in the gym, she was reading, journaling, and writing down her academic goals for the year. She was doing arts and crafts. She was walking her dog and getting more sunlight. She was cooking healthy, home-cooked meals. The goal of injury rehab is not to go through the motions and become a drone, nor is it to become pain free. It is to level up, come back stronger and better, both physically and mentally. Injured girls need to stimulate, not stagnate.

CHAPTER 6: Sample Program or Daily Habits?

"There's no substitute for hard work. If you work hard and prepare yourself, you might get beat, but you'll never lose."

– Nancy Lieberman

In sport performance, weight loss, athletic pursuits, college dreams and more, people opt for the shortcuts. They want the glory without the grind. They want the result without the actionable steps. They want the overnight success without the daily habits. They want the social media post without the effort behind the scenes. I know this is a tough pill to swallow, but girls need to master the basics first before they do the fanciest program out there, once a week, for a finite amount of time. As high-performance coach Nick Grantham beautifully states, "an advanced program is nothing if someone cannot adhere to it."

Moreover, let us build a culture of consistency and the work it takes to reach the next level. A program that female athletes stick to for months, years and beyond, that focuses on the basics – coordination, mechanics, strength, power, and balance, and all with good technique – goes way further than a program that is flashy, and is usually one where people only give half effort. I see this all the time: guru trainers taking on young girls, where the standard is *'just come and go as you please!'* or *'it's okay to train once a week!'* or *'here is my drop-in rate!'*

It is sad, to say the least. There is no accountability. No consistency. No good habits. No long-term development. Just money pocketed on a Sunday afternoon for a single session. Furthermore, paying money for a trainer is not wrong, but if the standard aligns with the quick fix culture and no real effort over time, I would be concerned where my money is going. Adding on, I would be worried about the message this is sending to the young female athlete: that inconsistency leads to high performance. That popping in and out and being flaky gets you far in life. That minimal effort gets life changing results. That not putting in the work makes you successful.

If a trainer brushes off missed workouts, that is a problem. If a trainer is not transparent about a 3-month minimum to see results, that is a problem. If a trainer promotes just showing up when athletes want, that is a problem. If a trainer accepts the parent who says, "let us have her try it once to see if she likes it," is a problem.

If a parent of a daughter is going in with reluctance, chances are, they are scared to commit and do not want to get better. A parent should not have to cajole his/her daughter into training. They should be ready to rock. Personally, I have had to get rid of clients because they couldn't commit to the process of physical development – one that takes several months, and years, to see beautiful results. If someone wants to increase speed, for example, we are about to be mastering the basics of coordination, mechanics, vertical forces, strength and power for a year at minimum. Even after a year and the speed times have improved, the real work is about to begin. It is not over once drastic improvement is made. Performance training in high school and college for female athletes becomes a much more challenging pursuit. A skill like speed will take even more training variability, detailed mechanics, and greater strength to improve by the millisecond.

Across the board, every athlete who began with me in middle school, saw a tremendous improvement in acceleration, speed, strength and lower body power in high school and college. These athletes mastered the basics from middle school until high school, twice a week speed training at minimum. Never did we ever do anything revolutionary. Never did we ever reinvent the wheel. Never did we ever do cool things just to get social media followers. Simply put, we mastered the basics and made these daily habits. **Hammering down the basics is a subtle art that overnight success seekers forget about.**

I like to compare this all to habits everyone learns from childhood:

- ➢ Brushing our teeth
- ➢ Making our beds
- ➢ Washing our hands
- ➢ Going to school
- ➢ Doing our homework
- ➢ Saying "please" and "thank you"
- ➢ Hydrating
- ➢ Eating our fruits and veggies

Of course, some people roll their eyes at these tasks, and many do not get excited about them, but since they were instilled at a young age, they are executed as second nature in adult life. These basics keep our hygiene, cleanliness, academic performance, character and everything else in check. The mundane is magical, and it is what girls must master in order to reach amazing heights in performance, career, and academics.

My College All-American Story: The Quintessence of Commitment

As a young soccer player, I had grit. Never was I satisfied, even when I was doing well and ahead of my teammates. Throughout middle school, I saw the drastic benefits of my speed, strength and conditioning program that when I reached high school freshman year, trying out for varsity did not phase me. I felt so robust, so explosive, and so confident in my ability to go up against the gigantic senior girls and absolutely crush it. Years of hard work in middle school allowed me to shine and make varsity soccer as a freshman. Mind you, I was second leading goal scorer my debut high school season.

After such a successful first year, I did not get complacent the following off-season. I continued to sharpen my skills, raise my speed and strength thresholds, and push past lung burning conditioning drills. In my sophomore, junior and senior years of high school, I still started, was one of the top goal scorers, and even was an All-State Player as well as County Player of the Year. During this time, I also was on the top club team in the state of Maryland, Bethesda Rapids, and was sought out by Division I programs like George Washington University, University of Wisconsin, and University of Maryland. In the end, I opted for a Division III program, Johns Hopkins University, because I loved the team culture, the academic challenge, and the campus size.

Going into my college freshman season, I could have been cocky and complacent. I could have gone through the motions and not pushed myself in my preparation. After such a dazzling high school and club soccer career, I could have gone in thinking, "I'm a hot shot." Alas, I did not. The Summer off-season was yet another chance for me to level up and raise my physical threshold even more. I wanted to go into college pre-season in my best shape and prove to the coach I could earn a starting position. So, what did I do the summer leading up? I did my usual five days a week speed, strength and conditioning program for three months, and did not miss a single workout. On top of my physical preparation, I sharpened my technical and tactical skills by playing pick-up soccer twice a week with the boys. I knew that if I put myself in a faster paced, more physical, and more creative environment than what I'm used to, I would show up to the pre-season scrimmages with confidence. And I did.

First things first, as a freshman, I got in the top 3 on every pre-season fitness test, and still had gas left in the tank for our three-a-day, pre-season practice schedule. When we did scrimmages, it was the easiest thing I did. While other girls were exhausted from the earlier sessions, I plowed through with intensity. My freshman season at Johns Hopkins University was a magical one: I was a starter, leading goal scorer, had the most game-winning goals, made the All-Conference Team, and was voted team Most Valuable Player and Most Valuable Offensive Player. Fast forward to Sophomore year, I could have adopted the mindset of being a hot shot and not put in any work because I had already earned my spot and collected all these accolades. However, that was not how I operated in my soccer career. Rather, I saw each season as an opportunity to improve and get even stronger, faster and more skilled, so of course, I continued with my speed, strength and conditioning, played pick-up soccer with the boys, and added in some extra one-on-one drills against the boys. My sophomore year was similar – starting position, leading goal scorer, All-Conference Team, and MVP. It was also the year we made it to the Elite 8 in the NCAA tournament and were ranked in the top 10 nationally.

After all the magic of my underclassmen years, I did not know how much better I could get, but **I still refined my craft and enjoyed the continuous pursuit of improved performance**. I owe it to the early middle school years of strength training because I saw the immense power of adding new stimulus to the muscles to get stronger. The human body's capabilities are enchanting, and I never ceased to be amazed how one can always level up, become stronger, build power, reverse the aging process, or heal joint pain.

In Junior year at Johns Hopkins, I was leading goal scorer again, and was awarded NSCAA All-America and Scholar All-America. I became captain my Senior year, led the team to a 21-1 record breaking season, and broke the all-time goal scoring record as a midfielder. On top of that, I got National Midfielder of the Year, Johns Hopkins University Outstanding Female Athlete, as well as my second NSCAA All-American and Scholar All-America awards. Beyond the accolades, I was at the apex of my playing career and was my fittest and healthiest I had ever been. It was because of all of the hard work behind the scenes, that I was able to be fully immersed in the present moment in competition and feel invigorated in my soul. I felt that since I worked on strengthening myself as an individual, I was able to contribute to the greater power of the collective group that was my team, and it made me ooze joy each game. When female athletes are better at what they do, they have more fun and can play from the heart. They are so confident in their physical preparation and training they did on their own, that come game time, they are not anxious or "in their head." Instead, they play with flow, and they illuminate the field with their gems, and light up others around them.

I tell the story of my college career to urge every female athlete to continue to level up. Even when they are totally rocking it out, leading their teams, or outrunning opponents, there is still work to be done. On the other end, even when they have been doing a physical preparation program for all but three months and do not yet see the results, keep going. Physical development is not always pretty, and that should excite all female athletes as they go through their programs. Buckle up, because the journey lasts a lifetime. When girls go through their sport careers and life with enchantment, they can keep digging out the treasures within themselves and discovering how much they can continue to accomplish.

This is Not a Program Book

I was reluctant to provide a sample performance program in this book, so instead I'm going to get people rolling on actionable, daily habits that compound over time to give girls an edge. Motor skill learning happens with repetition over time, then with a sprinkle of variability to work new muscle groups. To summarize, it encompasses mastering the basics then layering on load with weight training and speed with power training. So why am I not including a sample program that walks everyone through a progression?

First, there are programs at everyone's fingertips that anyone can find on the internet. Second, I already have two programs published in PDF format that can be utilized year-round, with strength circuits, speed and agility days, off-season and in-season templates, sets and reps, recovery circuits, and progressions and regressions. In conjunction with my programs, I offer online consulting to athletes and coaches for female athlete performance, both on the individual and team level. I also have a phone app that has programs all outlined and are extremely user friendly. At the same time, I can write the most jaw dropping performance plan with all the x's and o's, set and rep schemes, and progressions that get results, but if girls are not mentally ready to make a drastic transformation, they will not stick to it. The program, then, becomes useless.

There are many who don't want to make the commitment, both at the athlete and coach level.

It is because it is **hard**.

Building the youth female athlete takes an immense amount of consistency from the girls, and it takes years for coaches to learn how to apply the science in a practical setting. Admittedly, I'm over a decade into my career of training girls and I'm still solving the puzzle. I understand why coaches feel both incompetent and not confident in this space. Alas, this is what it takes to serve youth female athletes, so everyone needs to start now. It is tantamount to learning financial management, real estate, statistics, economics, and all the subject matter needed to thrive and survive in life. It takes time, effort, and relentless consistency.

A physical preparation program for female athletes needs to be executed year-round, and this is where coaches and organizations struggle. With that said, let us start with the daily, non-negotiable habits that girls can do at practices and or at home:

- Crawling
- Hanging
- Skipping
- Squatting
- Hinging
- Marching
- Balancing
- Hopping
- Throwing
- Jumping
- Walking
- Nasal Breathing

Why These Movements Are Crucial

When one looks at these movements, they are far from fancy. They are simple, utilize minimal equipment, and return the girl back to using her body as the strong machine that she was born with. Bear crawling, skipping, and hanging, for example, are the easiest movements young female athletes can do daily to bolster their coordination and strength, and they were the first movements they taught themselves. Yes, movement is self-taught, and it is a blessing how innately powerful the brain and body are. When girls were babies, they did not have trainers (or their parents) instructing them how to crawl, coordinate the opposite arm and leg, and activate their neck, shoulder and core strength to hold their heavy heads up. A baby's head, mind you, makes up 25% of their weight when born, which is a significant amount for a young one to hold up. It is downright impressive how a newborn navigates the world with such heaviness, and can still get around through crawling, rolling, then eventually walking. Another magical feat a baby is born with is the ability to hang from a bar. Of course, if any parent is going to try this with their newborn, they need to be sure to have a spotter for when the baby lets go. Try it and see how long they can hang because their grip can get them close to a minute hanging from the bar. The human hand has thousands of nerve endings that builds connection between the two brain hemispheres. With the growing technological culture, female athletes are moving away from using their hands and building their grip strength. The research shows that girls must return to what they were born with, and that grip strength is an indicator of longevity, and decline in grip strength is associated with an increased risk of mortality (1). The studies in this space are overwhelming, and on top of that, babies were born to boast their grip strength immediately, so it must be important for human survival.

Movement is what girls are born with, so they better not lose their ability to do the basics well – to coordinate their opposite limbs, to stabilize their cores, to walk, to sprint. The simple needs to be addressed repeatedly from cradle to grave. The thousands and thousands of "brush strokes" with these daily habits accumulate and contribute to better coordination, balance, stability and body control when girls perform higher intensity drills at training. Young female athletes should not go through the motions; they need to have an unsatiable desire to do the humdrum basics and not succumb to the quick fix culture. With anything in life – dieting, investing money, building a career – short-term thinking leads to long-term disaster. For example, the instant gratification from a 30-day detox, only to relapse and gain all the weight back; or the dopamine hit from buying a nice car, only to have buyer's remorse, a large monthly payment and a smaller bank account; or the girl who wants to do that fancy exercise for the split-second pleasure from a social media post, will be the one later in life signing up for all the New Year's weight loss gimmicks that prey on women's emotions. Or the girl who wants to rush from bodyweight movements straight to the barbell will be the girl who earns quick cash and loses her all her money from not investing. In most cases, short-term thinking does not work. Rather, long-term thinking and planning are far more sustainable in all facets of life, and the same applies to exercise and building muscle – the more a girl is committed to mastering the basics, the more likely she will stay healthy and be able to load safely.

Again, this is not a program book; it is to light a fire within everyone's souls first – to hammer home what young girls need, and to be clear on how significant this all is for them in sports and life. Daily habits are the first step to inspiring girls to take charge of their physical ability and long-term health. Always compound the basics over time to build physical health.

The Not Enough Time to do the Basics Excuse

If girls spend an average of 4-6 hours on their mobile device a day, or if they know every character from their favorite reality show, they can find time to work out. Life is about priorities, and girls will learn this harsh lesson as they get older, enter college, and the workspace. Incorporating daily physical habits into life isn't hard, so that's the good news. Girls can start with something as easy as balancing on one leg daily while brushing their teeth. They will build better proprioception in their foot to improve balance and be able to progress to harder, loaded balance work, such as Single Leg Deadlifts or Single Leg Squats. Another idea is to do bear crawls daily, even if it's in the living room between TV commercial breaks, or to skip to the bus stop instead of walking to work on hip flexibility, arm action and ball of foot strike for speed. Sitting on the floor, rather than in a chair, is another viable option to improve the flexibility of the hips. There are so many ways to get creative and add good movement habits into a girl's day, and these are so easy they don't interrupt everyday life.

The "Too Much" In-Season Scare

This is one of the biggest reasons coaches and parents are turned off by doing extra movement and strength training year-round. They feel the loading is too much on the body and will make girls sore and fatigued come game time.

Newsflash: it is not the strength training that is doing it. For field and court sports (lacrosse, field hockey, soccer, basketball, volleyball), the bad actor here is the eccentric loading (when the muscles rapidly lengthen and must contract to handle force) which happens during deceleration from cutting, jumping and changing of direction. So, if these dynamic movements are the most taxing, then what **isn't?**

Strength training is what prepares girls for taxing, eccentric movements, so they do not end up with a pulled muscle or torn ligament. It can be hard to peep in another activity such as speed and strength training, given the jam-packed nature of year-round sports. Many athletes and parents are going 3-4x a week to practices, and to tournaments on the weekends. This results in packing to-go meals, commuting copious amounts of miles, and at the same time, trying to maintain their sanity. Because of this overwhelm, physical preparation is the first thing parents cut from the schedule.

Of course, I understand how busy and overwhelming this all can get, but I also understand and feel it's my duty to be transparent with everyone: year-round speed and strength training is a must if we want young female athletes to do the following:

➤ Improve speed
➤ Reduce injury risk

- ➢ Stay resilient to overuse and over-training
- ➢ Improve movement quality and change of direction
- ➢ Withstand the demands of the game (deceleration, sprints, jumps, and cuts)

When it comes to in-season workout templates, the good news is, they do not need to be extensive. The solution is magically simple and saves an immense amount of time. First and foremost, I recommend young athletes see an in-person performance coach, but if the time spent driving to their facility is too much during the season, in-season workouts can be easy to execute at home or at the neighborhood playground.

Again, return to the daily movements, and once ready for more, add in the loaded movement patterns – Squats, Deadlifts, Pull-Ups, Push-Ups, and Lunges. In-season workouts should leave the athlete feeling good and energized, not sore and defeated. Therefore, the sets and reps should remain low and admittedly, I do not venture over 6 reps.

Encouraging girls to get their priorities straight and develop an organized routine for strength training will help them to stay healthy in-season. Too, it teaches them discipline in busy times. Because guess what? When they grow older and enter the real world, they're going to have to make their physical health a priority. Teach them these consistent habits young, while also urging them how critical it is to have a routine.

One of my favorite ways to fit in in-season workouts is to shorten them to 30 minutes by pairing an upper body and lower body exercise. Here is a sample routine:

A. Single Leg RDL 3x6

B. Floor Press 3x6

C. Pull-Up 4x5

D. RFE Split Squat 3x5

Female athletes can execute this by pairing exercises A and B together, then pairing C and D as supersets. An in-season routine like this should not take more than 15 minutes. If she wants to divide it up further, she can do the first two movements, then do some homework in between, then do the other two movements later that evening. There are no excuses to skip an in-season workout this short, especially if girls have time to peruse social media for a few hours a day.

The Fear of Too "Bulky"

"But I do not want to get bulky," a phrase uttered by many female athletes. It is one of the top reasons young girls are reluctant to get under the iron. There are many layers to peel back in this discussion – the way parents talk about body image, what is said in school, or what is seen as "ideal" on social media. Societal expectations and what the mainstream labels as "a fit body" can jostle any girl's psyche as she grows into her physique.

Even Serena Williams, one of the greatest female tennis players to ever live, has received heavy criticism regarding her athletic build. "Too thick" or "big" or "manly" have been some of the comments thrown her way. This breaks my heart because she is the quintessence of a strong and powerful woman, who has proven herself over and over in tennis. If Serena did not have her amazing muscles and athleticism, she would not be one of the most spectacular female tennis athletes of all time.

It is troublesome out there for female athletes, adult and young, because their bodies will be nitpicked no matter who it is. If a female athlete is too "bulky," she gets hate. If she is too skinny, she gets hate. If she is too short or tall, she gets hate. If she is too muscular, she gets hate. "Bulky" is an interesting term, but what does it mean? STRONG? ATHLETIC? MUSCULAR? Is it a term that birthed from the bodybuilding community, and young female athletes are afraid they will look like bodybuilders? Female athletes can rest assured that it takes an immense amount of volume (tons of sets and reps), isolation work, two workouts a day, meal timing, extra calories compared to the normal woman, and illegal performance enhancers (which I do not recommend EVER) to look like a bodybuilder. Too, female athletes who play sports that cover a lot of mileage (5-6 miles a match for soccer players, and then add on the 2-4 practices a week) are getting enough endurance work to offset excessive muscle gain and the "bulkiness" they fear.

"Bulky" is also a highly unique and vague concept. Every female athlete will put on muscle differently. Some may get more definition in their shoulders, some their hamstrings, some their hips, and this depends on their overall stature – height and bone structure. To help girls tackle the "bulky" problem, I focus on performance. Revisiting the physical tests mentioned earlier in this book is so important in this process. Are they improving their strength, speed and power numbers with consistent weight training? Do they feel more confident on the pitch? Do they have increased energy levels? Do they have improved mood and focus? Putting on muscle is not only good for performance, but is excellent for overall health.

Strength Doesn't Slow Girls Down

It only adds more to the engine.

Research suggests that there is a strong correlation between maximal strength and sprint times. The stronger the athlete is, the faster they will be. Speed is about being able to produce more force, and in order to achieve that, there needs to be more muscle on the body. Even during an 8-week in-season resistance training program performance indicators, such as acceleration, speed, jumping, and ball power, can be significantly improved in soccer players (2). In female softball players, "bodyweight and relative strength have strong correlations with speed and change of direction." (3)

This is a great segue into the next tool: *power training*. Building explosiveness involves training the components along the force velocity curve, wherein the middle lies power. In order to build a powerful female athlete, one cannot just train one end of the curve. Some train strength with no sprint work, while others train speed with no strength work. Training should encompass all pieces along the curve in order to optimize and find the golden middle of power output. Once this is attained, lifting weights does not make female athletes slow. The blend of getting under iron with explosive jumps and max effort sprint work on the pitch is the way to go for best results. Speed and strength are a powerful duo because one changes the game and leads to goal scoring (speed), while the other, keeps athletes in the game and maintains injury resiliency (strength).

Is Strength Training Safe?

Let me ask this: is going for a head ball safe? Is going for a tackle safe? Is jumping safe? Is pushing and shoving safe? Is changing direction safe?

The most aggressive actions in sports rarely get questioned, while supervised weight training does. It is comical, to say the least. "I do not want her to get injured," a parent remarks about lifting weights, thinking it is going to be a bootcamp or CrossFit class that will obliterate their daughter. "I don't want it to stunt her growth," another parent comments. Nothing could be further from the truth, if the right people are teaching youth female athlete resistance training. The problem is not weight training being unsafe; **the problem is not weight training enough to stay safe in sports**. As the physical demands continue to amount – harder tackles, more changes of direction, more high-speed running and miles covered, the training on the back end needs to be done even more to build a robust female athlete.

Strength training is safe when taught by a professional and progressed accordingly to maintain an athlete's strength in-season. Providing that the performance coach is teaching the main movements well, and the girls are not throwing their backs out during loaded deadlifts and squats, resistance training is incredibly safe and beneficial to the youth female athlete.

Coaches Damaging Female Athletes

Team coaches are increasingly taking on the role of the performance coach, and while their intention is genuine, they are not giving exercises appropriate for the health of the female athlete. Even if a female athlete is seeing a performance coach outside of her team sessions, what her coach does at practices can be damaging her body and hindering her progress. Too many times, I have heard my girls tell me their coaches are running them through "fitness circuits" and doing "injury prevention." I then ask what these workouts entail, and I get things like hundreds of box jumps, burpees, frog hops and a plethora of plyometric drills that give the illusion that girls are being productive.

I cannot help but ask these questions:

Was technique taught?

Are the girls executing these movements with quality?

Is there a rhyme or reason behind the number of sets and reps given?

Is there a specific adaptation being achieved?

Is the goal muscle soreness and fatigue?

Performance training does not just lie in the hands of the performance coach, but the team coach, too. After all, female athletes see them more than their strength coach. This is not to say the team coach must run a revolutionary weight room session on the pitch, but they need to sprinkle in glimpses of balance, coordination, stability and deceleration work. This can be done during the warm-up in just under ten minutes every time the female athlete goes to team practice. Female athletes can march, skip, crawl, jump, land, decelerate, and accelerate in warm-up, and this compounds over time to build them into more efficient movers.

Coaches need to stop with the endless cacophony of random exercises that have no meaningful adaptation, except to make girls sweat and the parents to "ooh" and "ahh." Here is what all coaches need to stop programming now at practices:

Russian Twists

Burpees

Sit-ups

High Volume Squat Jumps, Push-Ups, Broad Jumps with poor execution

Long Slow Distance Runs

This list is just the tip of the iceberg when it comes to catastrophic movements for female athletes. These are problematic because they do not focus on building the stability of the trunk, the ability to absorb force and control momentum, and the strength of the posterior chain. Sit-ups, as an example, are the worst core exercise programmed for growing girls. When they are in their growth spurt, their spine is growing at a rapid rate, with standing height increases by 1.4 to 1.5 cm/year. It is for this reason that majority of spinal deformities tend to exacerbate drastically during puberty (4). What sit-ups do to the spine is they place stress on the lumbar region because they get it out of its natural curve. Instead, female athletes need to work on strengthening the low back muscles, as well as their trunk area (gluteal muscles, obliques, anti-rotation of anterior core) in order to support the health of the spine. The spine is not a force producer, but rather force absorber. Sit-ups are not transferrable to the actions in female sports either. When a soccer player rockets a shot, she does not hunch over or flex her spine. Instead, it remains upright and stable so the hip flexor can be mobile enough to follow through on her shot. When she is holding off defenders, she is also stabilizing her trunk area, not flexing it. Every exercise a coach programs in practice must have transfer behind it, as well as look out for the health of the female athlete.

CHAPTER 7: Causes of Female Athlete Injuries People Ignore

"Being relentless means demanding more of yourself than anyone else could ever demand of you, knowing that every time you stop, you can still do more. You must do more."

– Tim Grover

Tim Grover, Kobe Bryant's trainer, said Kobe was the best at his sport because he did more than what was expected. Beyond his training, he zeroed in on his sleep, nutrition and stress management. When injuries are connected to only physical deficits, the result is a disservice to every female athlete.

"Her hips are weak!"

"Her hips are wide!"

"She didn't warm-up properly!"

"Her quad to hamstring ratio is off!"

At this point, these are obvious statements. While hip imbalances, body structures, and improper warm-ups play massive roles, they're only a sliver of the cause of injury pie. There is always more – more to improve, more to build, more to work on, more to dial in on – that impacts the musculoskeletal and nervous systems. Looking at the top athletes in the world, they are engrossed in their regimens – how they eat, how they manage stress, how they hydrate, how they recover – because they know if they fall short with any of these, game-changing errors, injuries can occur. Alex Morgan, for example, is painstaking with her nutrition and only eats food that makes her feel energized, namely anti-inflammatory fruits and veggies. She says, "I feel like what you put in your body is the energy and output you're going to get so that's very important for athletes."

When coaches, trainers and parents peep into a young female athlete's lifestyle and private life off the field, the fully story of her decreased performance, or increased injuries, comes to the surface.

Too Much Tech

The first component beyond training that can impact performance and increase injury risk is too much staring at mobile devices and laptops. I grew up in the time of AOL Instant Messenger, screen names, and flip phones, and began to see the unfolding of the tech addiction and the damage from chasing dopamine. Getting a new friend request on messenger made me feel giddy, and seeing a text on my Nokia flip phone made my eyes light up. When I did not receive a message for days, my stomach began to knot, and my anxiety began to creep in because that feel good moment what not being fed to me.

Today, the endless scrolling, the flashing pop up ads, the blue light exposure, and the stimulating videos are ruining young girls. The extent of this problem is so complex it is hard for many to comprehend. People simply are not aware of the mental and physical damage that is occurring from staring at screens for hours on end. Girls are getting in a lot of reps from the stress of blue light: on average, pre-teen girls spend 6 hours a day on their phones, and teenagers are spending 9 hours a day. For a youth female athlete who has a 24-hour day to get her sleep, train for her sport, recover, prepare healthy meals, do homework, and make time for leisure, social media can be a time-consuming distraction. **Spending hours captivated by her glowing screen is surely taking away precious time that could be spent doing things that boost her health and enrich her life.**

Let us start with the effect on the nervous system. Many young girls are rarely taking a break from the noise, with the constant scrolling, group messaging, responding to texts, being available all the time, and staring at the blue light for days. They are always in a sympathetic "fight or flight" state, causing her brain to be fatigued and unable to do its job come game-time. When the nervous system has exhausted its ability to function at 100%, it will fail to fire the muscles that safeguard the joints, and this causes the body to go back to faulty biomechanics and slow information processing (excessive knee valgus, anterior pelvic tilt, trunk instability, poor balance, and slow reaction time).

Bear in mind that social media is just like food; both are forms of consumption and can uplift or a damage female athlete. What girls consume, is who they become as athletes and humans. The liking, the scrolling, the clicking, and the commenting all impact a girl's internal state, just as food does the same thing. But instead of impacting the digestive system, **social media impacts the *nervous system.*** The swirl of distractions not only stresses out a young girl's brain, but it takes her away from truly understanding what she needs. She has outsourced her mental state to a device that disappoints her time and time again because it comes at the expense of neglecting herself. She forgets how to listen to her body. She slacks with her training. She is so painfully unaware that she forgets to pour love into herself. She looks to an itty-bitty six-inch screen for health advice, dating tips, entertainment, and fulfillment that feeds their emptiness. Her attention is transfixed on the ten second video clips, the flashes, the music, and is constantly fed information. She barely knows herself. Susceptible to the dopamine hit, she is an easy target for ongoing distraction and her attention is no longer her own. She is held back from taking charge of her own life. She does not know herself, and she becomes insecure since she is constantly looking outside herself for approval. Her mind gets jerked around at all hours of the day, and she loses her sovereign control over her thoughts and actions.

Is this how we want young girls to grow up and evolve? To plop on a sofa and be engrossed by blue light? To be constantly anxious and sympathetically driven? To be fed 50 notifications, have multiple apps, and five social media accounts? To be so seduced by technology that it isolates them from family and friends? To be so frozen by a device that they ignore movement and their physical health? To seek external validation from Likes and Comments? To be distracted and ignore their creative power and inner gems?

NO.

Female athletes are here to create, connect, play, experience, rest, move, adapt, move more, see their strengths, and know their bodies are capable of amazing things. After all, these are actions that give youth female athletes their vitality. Many believe their girls need more trainers, drills, coaching, speed training, track workouts, sessions, and more, more, more. They truly need less; less of the noise that is keeping their nervous systems amped up, which results in being unable to show up focused, motivated, and infused with clarity and creativity. They need narrowed focus and consistency.

This is a call to action: girls need to make social media fasting a part of their performance program. First, they should set a goal of eliminating it for a few hours a day; then slowly increasing that to several hours a day, then trying to go off social media for an entire week. Decreasing the number of hours that they are slouched over, head forward, and eyes glazed at a screen, does wonders for the nervous system, and gets female athletes back into the "rest and digest" parasympathetic state. Among other things, their anxieties will wither away because they are not continually seeking more and more stimulation. This is a recovery solution far better than slapping on an ice bag because it addresses internal neurological issues that cause muscles to tighten up.

The break from this sympathetic state is one way to mitigate performance anxiety. Our ancestors only entered a "fight or flight" state when there was something life threatening while they were out hunting. This isn't to discount the anxiety young girls feel, but in the first world, we rarely face these life-or-death situations. **Taking a break from social media is one of the first steps to helping with anxiety.**

Expounding more on the amazing benefits of less tech, is to bolster the immune system. When girls are in a stressed-out state most of their day, their immune systems become compromised. Remember: the key to a successful sports career is a healthy one. It would be a shame if a girl got sick during a major recruiting tournament, or a championship game, or her senior day. We want girls healthy in their muscles, bones and joints, but also in their immune systems. Girls need to wean themselves away from social media. When they do this, notice how vibrant they become.

Lack of Nourishment and Fuel

Before my off-season training morning sessions, I would ask my female athletes, "What did you have for breakfast?" They always replied, "a banana."

Wrong answer.

This is a common scenario amongst all female athletes – they are not getting enough fuel through food. In my conversations with my Registered Dietician colleagues, they tell me they do not know many girls who are meeting their energy requirements. This is catastrophic because girls are growing at such a rapid rate during adolescence that their muscles and bones are starving for macronutrients, vitamins and minerals. Even young women in college sports need nourishment to sustain the heavier demands of their sports, early morning weight room sessions, the oscillating sleep schedules, the stressors from academics, and the rigors of fitness testing.

The older girls, especially, cannot get away with error in their nutrition. Most think they are still young and invincible, but they're not. I saw this firsthand when one of my girls from University of North Carolina Women's Soccer, a division 1 soccer powerhouse, came home during holiday break and was preparing for her brutal conditioning test. She asked me to time her during the test, and by the time she was near the end and over 60 repeated sprints deep, she began to lose her fire. She churned and barely made it through. When wrapping up the test, I saw her cross the finish line in exhaustion and pain, only to see her then walk over to the sideline to puke all over the field. For a young woman who was in tremendous shape and dialed in with her physical training the entire off-season, I was confused as to why the test destroyed her so much. So, I dug deeper and asked her, "what did you eat before this?" She answered, "I ate tacos an hour before this." I replied, "big mistake," with a stern look on my face. She nodded in agreement and said she learned her lesson.

Physical training is all well and good, but **it is the nutrition that makes a good athlete become unstoppable**. Anytime a parent asks me how their girl can get an edge, I always say, "have her out-nourish, out-hydrate, and out-fuel her opponents." Proper nutrition is crucial for sports, and it is also a lifetime game that needs to be taught to girls young, not just by trainers like me. Of course, I pride myself in walking the walk with my own nourishment and leading by example for my female athletes. There have been many sessions I have brought healthy snacks, fruits, and electrolyte-infused drinks for the girls to try, with the hopes of inspiring them to take care of their bodies. There have been sessions in the gym where I was so busy, I still had healthy meals prepared and protein shakes to imbibe on the job. There have been times I have gone out to eat with my athletes and I always order my go-to salad with a quality protein like fish or chicken. Beyond that, I have sent group texts to my girls to share a healthy meal they cooked and that might inspire the rest of the group to do the same.

As much as I try to lead by example on nutrition, as well as have weekly discussions with my athletes, this is not enough to elicit drastic nutritional behavior change. Female athletes spend around 4-6 hours a week with their coaches and trainers, but where are they the rest of the time? *At home with their parents.*

Over the years, parents would ask me to change their girl's food habits, and believed I was the panacea to getting them to stop eating fast food. I can suggest eating all the veggies in the world and drop science on why female athletes need vitamin D, calcium, carbohydrates, and protein for muscle growth and recovery. However, when a girl is in a household with only toxic sludge, what I recommend becomes totally meaningless.

Proper nutrition starts in the household. **I repeat proper nutrition starts in the household.**

The mom who drinks a can of Coke every night and polishes off a frozen pizza is not exemplary eating behavior. The dad who orders fast food every night is also not the best inspiration. The pantry that is stocked with processed foods is not the optimal environment to be exposed to every day.

Do parents really think a trainer is going to salvage their daughter when it comes to proper nutrition? Young female athletes look up to adults, but their parents play the biggest role in their nutrition. They are the ones buying the groceries. They are the ones in charge of the domestic economy. They are the ones putting the meals on the dinner table. Notwithstanding what has just been said, "you are a product of your environment" cannot ring truer.

Sadly, **this triggers many parents because they are not willing to admit they're enabling negative eating behavior.** The first step to changing the food environment in the household is admitting there is a problem, and the meals are not serving the female athlete's performance. The second step is to understand that eating healthy can be cheap and easy. It does not have to be expensive, and no, people do not have to eat Acai bowls that cost $13 a pop, nor do they have to buy all organic. Though I recommend getting the highest quality meat from a pasture-raised farm, provide your girl with enough protein, and ensure she is consuming all the essential amino acids from chicken, beef, turkey, and fish first. A general rule of thumb is a quarter of a plate of protein, and a half plate of carbohydrates (rice, pasta, quinoa, sandwich). The next step is to give her a fist-full of vegetables and fruit at every meal, so she is infusing her body with vitamins, minerals, and hydration. Speaking of hydration, plain water does not do the job, yet the water industry is flooded with brands that are a joke. Go to the supermarket and there is a myriad of water types – alkaline, spring, pH, and Icelandic glacier water. The water industry has had a field day telling athletes they are not hydrated enough and that their magic formula will solve dehydration.

What the water folks are not being honest about is when athletes sweat, they lose more than water - minerals such as magnesium, potassium, zinc, iodine, and copper. Therefore, sports drinks entered the market to then claim they knew the solution. While some sport drinks have the electrolytes needed to replenish lost minerals, they also have copious amounts of sugar in them for added flavor, and added chemicals for a picturesque, vibrant color. Some athletes might thrive off and need this sugar, but it is up to the girl to figure that out for herself. When an athlete is depleted of electrolytes, her cognitive ability declines – focus, energy, motivation, and reactivity – and adding sugar could cause an inevitable crash for some. Many girls I have worked with have told me conventional sports drinks also give them cramps and it is painful to finish the second half of a game. The best things a youth female athlete can do for hydration and energy are the following: hydrate with fruit and vegetables, due to their high-water content, as well as high vitamins and minerals content for a massive bang-for-buck. Second, they can make their own sports drink at home and know all the ingredients inside without added sugar and chemicals. My favorite recipe includes eight ounces of water, one or two freshly squeezed lemons, a dash of pink sea salt, and a quarter cup of honey. Everyone might have to play around with these ratios to get the desired taste.

Making nutrition fun and family oriented is the best way to elicit change. Again, it needs to be a household event and I urge families to make their own hydration drinks and cook their own meals. Sitting down for a family dinner has been lost in the on-the-go and quick-fix, fast food culture, but it is a necessity for connection, good health, and consistent habits. If girls can get on board with proper nutrition in their early years, it is more likely they will stay disciplined when the ante is upped in college and professional sports. **If the performance goals of a female athlete are high-level, she needs to eat at a high level.** When her sports career ends, she will also be equipped with the tools to keep her body healthy for a lifetime. Hippocrates had it right: "let food be thy medicine."

Poor Recovery…Stop Icing Muscles!

A female athlete is as strong as her recovery. If girls truly understand and are cognizant of the value of recovery, they will stand out above the rest, perform at a high level, stay healthy, and improve all areas of their lives. However, recovery gets butchered all the time. Ask any girl what they do to recover, they say things like "ice, cryotherapy, massage, or go for a jog."

Let me address ice first. Icing an injury does not speed up the internal healing process. It is a temporary relief and numb to the pain, that is not worth it in the long run if an athlete wants to get blood flow to the injured area, and produce more insulin-like growth factor to boost muscle repair. For a more severe injury like a knee sprain, it needs blood flow so that it can begin the healing process. Too, the joint also needs nutrients like protein and collagen so that the integrity of the joint becomes stronger. Adding on, the knee needs the muscles that safeguard it to become stronger than they were prior to injury. **Icing does not make a joint more durable, nor does it make a joint more protected.**

My recommendation would to be elevate the injured area but begin to contract the muscles around it immediately. Or if it is something like an ankle sprain, the joint can be moved a tiny bit to facilitate healing. Even if it is a few millimeters at a time, the tissues need blood flow and oxygen delivery to begin to repair. Female athletes with injured ankles can slowly write the ABCs with the joint to gain some mobility back. Of course, when a female athlete has an ankle sprain, she can still see her strength coach and train around the area by doing Pull-Ups, Push-Ups, Pistol Squats, and Deadlifts, so long as she is cleared by her Physical Therapist.

Stop Popping Pills

Next up, pill popping needs to stop. Any time a girl suffers an injury or experiences pain, they bolt to the cabinet and pop a Motrin, Ibuprofen, or Tylenol. When an athlete has an acute injury, the first thing an adult suggests is "take a Motrin!" Nonsteroidal anti-inflammatory drugs are terrible for a child. More studies are showing these pills delay bone and connective tissue healing. Sure, they might alleviate a temporary moment of pain, but looking at the long-term, they disrupt the natural healing process (1). Adding on to the disaster, these drugs can impact digestive health which can cause disrupted sleep and a compromised immune system (2). The gut, in fact, is the driver of the immune system, so if it is not functioning properly and getting rid of waste, the immune system becomes compromised. In addition, it is correlated to skin health, so for girls who do not want acne, but want glowing skin, they better be looking after the well-being of their gut.

Instead of taking pills, to facilitate the natural healing process, girls can opt for foods packed with collagen, amino acids, B vitamins, and vitamin C. Collagen is a crucial protein that helps with joint repair and tissue strength. B vitamins help with muscle growth as well as repair, and vitamin C helps the body produce collagen, and protects cells from damage from free radicals. These sources are packed with the nutrients a female athlete craves to be more nourished, hydrated, energized, and recovered.

Stop Jogging

The worst of all these recovery methods is jogging – a method that both overloads and slows the down female athlete. The truth is, she already ticks the aerobic box by going to practices and games. Also, if she is doing her daily walking or playing outside with friends, she gets enough endurance work. If parents want their girl to be more robust, faster, stronger and more powerful, they would evade the long slow distance running altogether. **Jogging at slow speeds exposes their nervous system to more slow twitch muscle fiber recruitment and gets them into the jogging motor pattern that deprives them of speed development.** Adding to the catastrophe that is long slow distance running, girls are out of alignment after practices and games, with most of their sports being quadricep, hip flexor, and anterior dominant. It is best to not add more fuel to fire by running and continuing to load these faulty patterns and overused muscle groups. The takeaway is clear: **do not use long slow distance running as recovery. It is a disaster.**

Recovery is not popping pills, icing, getting your back oiled up and scratched, nor is it long distance running, or stepping into an ice chamber that costs a pretty penny. The modalities everyone gravitates toward for recovery are far from free and can put a dent into anyone's bank account. Parents who complain about the costs of playing youth sports are the first to opt for expensive recovery tools, when all the free ones are right in front of their eyes. **True recovery is simple, and it should put the body in the best position possible to return to a parasympathetic state so it can build itself back up again.** The goal is not to be numbed from pain or muscle soreness; the goal is to come back rested and robust.

Let me begin with the methods that can be executed with ease, with many of them being free healthcare.

Breathing

Ask any girl to take a deep breath and she will breathe in through her mouth and elevate her shoulders. Many girls today fail to breathe properly, and they are stuck in a sympathetic state with their nervous system on overdrive. **Here is what you need to know: the mouth is only for eating and drinking. The nose is for breathing.**

All female athletes need to try this: at rest or walking, put a minute on the clock and count how many breaths they take. If it is over 8, they are more sympathetic and not breathing slow enough. They want to aim for under 8 breaths, breathing through the nose slowly. When the breath goes through the nose it can go down to the diaphragm (rather than chest), which produces less oxidative stress and cortisol. Breathing properly through the nasal passageway through meditation, whether lying down or walking, increases the production of melatonin, an antioxidant, which helps with improving sleep.

One of the biggest pioneers in Integrative Medicine, Dr. Andrew Weil, invented the "4-7-8" breath method to help his patients regulate their breathing and slow their heart rates. He recommends breathing through the nose for a four second count, holding breath for seven seconds, then exhaling for eight seconds through the mouth. What this does is calms the nervous system and is a simple, yet effective method Dr. Andrew has used with his patients as prevention for disease. Calming the nervous system through slow breathing improves sleep, reduces inflammation, enhances muscle recovery, and improves cognitive function. He also states that over decades of seeing patients, this method of breathing is one of the best anti-anxiety medications, and prescribed anxiety medications are pathetic in comparison. (3)

Another expert on proper breathing, James Nestor, states in his book, "it turns out that when breathing at a normal rate, our lungs will absorb only about a quarter of the available oxygen in the air. Most of that oxygen is exhaled back out. By taking longer breaths, we allow our lungs to soak up more in fewer breaths. Mouth breathing, it turns out, changes the physical body and transforms airways, all for the worse. Inhaling air through the mouth decreases pressure, which causes the soft tissues in the back of the mouth to become loose and flex inward, creating less space and making breathing more difficult." (4) He is also a big supporter of breathing through the nose, and suggests it is incredibly beneficial for brain function for creative thought and critical thinking.

If female athletes can get their breathing right, everything becomes right:

- Strengthens the diaphragm
- Improves lung capacity
- Improves parasympathetic nervous system
- Improves sleep
- Increases exchange of oxygen and carbon dioxide
- Improves circulation
- Improves health of the teeth and gums
- Reduces inflammation

For something so simple, and free to do, it has a significant number of benefits. For the young girl who is overstressed and overstimulated, this is her greatest tool to regaining her sense of calm to speed up her recovery. Remember when I discussed the intelligence of babies and how they learn to move their bodies? Observe babies while they are sleeping and at rest: their mouths are closed, and are breathing through their noses.

I just let you in on the best kept secret: the first step to proper recovery is free. Close your mouth and breathe through your nose.

Sleeping

If I could choose my favorite recovery method, it would be sleep. Beyond having a strength deficit, sleep deprivation is the biggest cause of injury in female athletes. Girls need it to regain their energy, motivation, focus, and muscular strength. Both the brain and body replenish during the sleep cycles, most notably during deep slow-wave and REM sleep. During deep sleep, growth hormone is secreted, and the muscles rebuild, so everything that was done during the day – the training – was worth it. During REM sleep, the brain is most active, and dreams occur, which is a "cleaning out" of the brain for better memories and cognition. There is compelling evidence from EEG studies in youth measuring electrical activity of the brain that showed that bad quality sleep can impact neural function, hinder memory formation, and decrease learning ability (5).

Sleep deprivation is one of the biggest issues plaguing young athletes today - the amount of over-stimulation, over-stress, and under-nourishment causes a cyclical mess that hampers their sleep. Studies have shown that youth athletes are not getting enough sleep and obtain less than 8 hours of sleep regularly (6). This has been shown to have a significant impact on reaction time, strength, speed, cognitive learning, and decision making, as well as increasing injury risk. In a study of middle and high school athletes, Milewski et al found that individuals who got less than 8 hours per night were 70% more likely to suffer an injury, compared to those who slept more than 8 hours. In addition, a multivariate analysis showed that athletes who slept on average less than 8 hours per night were 1.7 times more likely to have suffered an injury (7). Another study points out that there are clear negative effects of sleep deprivation on performance, including reaction time, accuracy, vigor, submaximal strength, and endurance (8).

Sleep has a significant impact on sport performance, but most notably, brain development for learning and memory. The adolescent brain especially needs sleep so it can remodel properly, and optimize memory systems, socioemotional processing, and emotion regulation. This is a precarious time for the youth brain, and the focus needs to be on optimizing sleep (11). Knowing how damaging lack of sleep is for performance and injury, here is the winning line-up for youth female athletes to improve sleep:

- Stop technology use 60 minutes before bed time
- Dim the lights in the house two hours before bed
- Start the day with natural sunlight exposure
- Be exposed to the sun as much as possible during the day
- Consume foods rich with magnesium and vitamin C
- Consume high quality proteins with essential amino acids
- Practice daily mindfulness and meditation
- Utilize the "4-7-8" breathing method before bed for 5 minutes
- Master nasal breathing during the day

One more thing I want to touch on is the use of melatonin and other sleep medications. My blunt opinion: avoid these. Anything that masks symptoms and gets young girls away from their brain's natural sleep rhythm never bodes well. While melatonin is excellent for falling asleep quickly, it is not ideal for achieving deep sleep. Deep, slow-wave sleep is when growth hormone is produced, and the muscles can build back up again. Focusing on natural methods to fall asleep faster, such as mindfulness and meditation are the best way to go (9). The Sleep Foundation says that these methods are more effective than medications, and one study indicated meditation as an excellent treatment for long-term insomnia (12). Sleep is imperative for youth female athletes. The most rested girls are the most powerful, vibrant, motivated, and energized athletes.

Walking

I'm obsessed with walking.

It is a lost art because there are more conveniences – cars, elevators, escalators, and planes – that have hindered innate human movement. People have chosen to be in front of glowing screens that are right at their fingertips, rather than taking a stroll outside to admire nature. There is more sitting time in the eight hours of day at school, and female athletes suffer to relieve their tight hips and low back when they get home. "Just stretch!" is the common suggestion when girls are tight from school, and as I mentioned before, this is not going to solve the problem. The solution is that girls need to walk more outside of practices and games.

Walking is something that has been a constant for all human history, so it must be important for our continued evolution, both physiologically and neurologically. Our ancestors had to walk incredible distances to find food and survive. They had to walk miles on end to build communities and connect with other beings. Walking is in our DNA, and it is something that should not wither away so long as humans are on planet Earth.

If a female athlete is going to do any active recovery, it should be walking, not jogging. First and foremost, our ancestors expended energy sprinting, jumping, climbing, and a plethora of high intensity activities (like sports), and as recovery, they walked or went to bed. Why don't we do the same? Looking at the time span thousands of years is the best research study out there to speak to the power of walking for the human species. For those who are not convinced, today's literature supports the behavior of our ancestors. Since recovery is neurological, the activities girls do post-competition must activate the parasympathetic nervous system to decrease the stress response in the body. A study in *Environment and Behavior* indicated that walking lowers cortisol levels, but not just any walking. In a controlled study, the group who walked in nature, compared to the group who walked while watching nature scenes on TV, resulted in lower cortisol levels and improved mood (13). When I prepare my performance plans for my female athletes, I always write, "walk with no mobile device in nature" and I mean it. They think I am crazy, but when they try it, they report feeling relaxed and energized. When I ran one of my first performance camps back in 2013, the recovery week encompassed a series of nature walks, where we went hiking on flat ground and enjoyed each other's company. Not only was it a relaxing experience for the girls, but it was a bonding experience full of laughter and smiles, so I highly recommend team walking in nature as recovery for female athletes. There is something soothing about being present with human conversation, being immersed in the lusciousness of nature, and hearing the delicate sounds of a breeze blowing or a creek flowing, with no stimulation from a screen. More studies continue to come out on the benefits of nature walking, suggesting that a forest may promote relaxation by facilitating the parasympathetic nervous system (14).

Walking must also be done barefoot. I know this sounds earthy, but the benefits of being barefoot are incredible. For one, it spreads out the toes, which allows for a stronger base from which to move. It can also improve posture and balance in the body because it strengthens the muscles and ligaments in the foot. Female athletes should walk, and even strength train, barefoot. The more they can get out of over-supportive shoes or suffocating cleats that confine their feet, the better. This is a simple way to help them offset the chances of foot and ankle injuries, as well as avoid nagging bunions, heel pain, or plantar fasciitis that come from tight, restricted footwear.

Female athletes need to stop jogging and do more walking barefoot as recovery. Adding on to the benefits of walking, a girl is removing waste from the muscles and getting the desired neurological effect of a decrease in nervous system stress. Jogging is a more stressful recovery because the heart rate is more elevated. Additionally, after a game a girl's posture is out of alignment (tight hip flexors, inhibited posterior chain), and jogging would add more load to the disaster. On the other hand, walking allows the girl to be mindful of her posture, get the heart rate in a more rested state, and perform a non-impact activity for the muscles and joints. Adding onto the recovery benefits from walking, it also improves left and right brain connectivity, increases creativity, and soothes the soul. Better yet, have girls regain focus in their breath work, breathing slowly through the nose and aiming for less than eight breaths per minute. Don't forget to keep the mouth closed!

Eating Nutrient Dense Foods

This one was already covered in the nourishment section, but I am going to revisit it once more. I cannot implore female athletes enough to take their nourishment and fueling routines seriously. Muscles are sore after training and games because of all the microtrauma that accrues. Even when they don't experience soreness afterwards, their body is still incredibly broken down and in a catabolic state. In order to heal the body and return to equilibrium, the young girl needs to put fuel back into her muscles (protein, carbohydrates) and brain (healthy fats) so she can return even better for the next competition. **Recovery is all about building the female athlete back up.**

The brain is part of this discussion as well, because it consists of nearly 60-70 percent fat. Consuming fatty acids is of utmost importance for the brain to be able to perform. Most youth female athletes are severely deficient in omega 3 fatty acids, and lack of this essential nutrient impacts the brain's processing and memory, and can have profound impacts on mood. After a game, the brain is depleted due to making thousands of split-second decisions and being constantly stimulated by its environment. Just like the muscles, the brain needs nourishment for neural connections to build back up. The insulating sheaths of the neurons rely on long-chain fatty acids, docosahexaenoic acid (DHA) and arachidonic acid (AA). For optimal brain function, female athletes are best getting fat from fatty fish — salmon, mackerel, anchovies — and eggs, organ, and muscle meats. If girls are not getting enough DHA in their diet, then supplementing with a high-quality fish oil is a viable option.

Beyond athletic performance, omega-3 fatty acids are involved in the prevention of some aspects of cardiovascular disease, and in some neuropsychiatric disorders, such as depression and Alzheimer's disease (15). Feeding the brain is crucial for performance and life, and young girls need to get on board now, so their brains do not wither away when they are older. Cognitive decline is inevitable as we age but can be offset with proper nutrients, and not shying away from fats. In fact, I encourage female athletes to load up on the eggs and pasture-raised bacon. High quality pork has twice the amount of Vitamin E, which is crucial for brain and hormonal health. It is packed with choline, which helps to reduce memory loss over time. Yes, high quality proteins are more expensive, but what can be cut out from the budget that is not serving the female athlete and the family? Greasy potato chips? High sugar cereals? Expensive iPads? Something has got to give. This reminds me: if parents are not setting the example, then girls will remain in their toxic eating patterns. Can parents return to the home cooked family dinners? Can parents feed their girls healthy fats that their bodies are starved for? Can parents also improve their own health along the way? You bet.

Another nutrient female athletes are deprived of is Vitamin D, which is plays a pivotal role in strong bone formation, as well as immune function. Several pediatric studies show there is solid evidence that vitamin D supplementation can reduce the rates of infections in pediatric populations. There is also growing evidence for a beneficial role of supplementation in preventing autoimmune disorders, and there is data linking vitamin D deficiency to increased rates of childhood asthma and other allergic conditions (16). Vitamin D deficiency can also hinder the structural integrity of the bones and joints, thus leaving girls more likely to suffer injuries, even if they are strength training. Yes, strength training will reduce chances of injury, but if Vitamin D isn't flooding into the bones, muscles and joints, the workout isn't as effective. Vitamin D is a potent nutrient that the upbuilds female athlete.

The last nutrient girls are deprived of is magnesium, which helps with regulating nerve function and blood pressure, and improving bone health (aids in Vitamin D and calcium absorption). When a female athlete is low on magnesium, she may feel tired or weak, and these symptoms may amplify when she's menstruating. Foods that are packed with magnesium are nuts (almonds, cashews, Brazil nuts), peanut butter, flax seeds, chia seeds, salmon, dark chocolate (yum!), kale, spinach, bananas, and oats. A bonus of magnesium is it is a muscle relaxer, so it is excellent for recovery and improved sleep. Magnesium Glycinate is one of the best supplements to aid insomnia, but please get it from food first before opting for supplementation.

If parents and coaches want their female athletes to get an edge, they would spend less money on cryotherapy and massage guns, and more on meals and snacks infused with nutrients that rebuild their bodies. The best snacks to have on deck after an intense training session or game are pre-made sandwiches with meat or eggs, veggies, avocado, tuna, cheese, or yogurt with fruit and nuts, or bread with yummy nut butters. Of course, this takes careful preparation before the weekend game madness, but isn't it worth nourishing female athletes, rather than having them starve for nutrients that support the systems in their body?

Stop Static Stretching

Young girls' muscles are not tight. They are weak.

There have been numerous times when I have been out watching soccer games and wandered around the sports complex to only see a team of female athletes touching their toes for a mundane, team stretch. Sadly, no one is truly stretching. When the coach says to circle up post-game, young girls are going through the motions while picking dandelions and chatting with their teammates. When I see static stretching happening pre-game, I want to bang my head into a wall. The reason muscles get tight is not due to physiology. It is due to neurology. When the brain is fatigued, it tightens up the muscles to protect them and their deep tissue. Think of it as the brain going into "defense mode." So, if the brain is at fault, then holding a muscle in a lengthened position is not going to do the trick; in fact, it could make matters worse. There are numerous studies that say static stretching inhibits muscular performance, reduces strength, weakens lower body stability, and can even impair explosive performance (17). It also doesn't help with reducing injuries like shin splints, sprains and strains, according to research from Clinical Journal of Sport Medicine (18).

One of the most common static stretches is reaching down to touch the toes. Don't get me started on the "my hamstrings are tight" nonsense. Alright, I already started. Here is what everyone needs to know: **most youth female athletes do not have tight hamstrings; rather, they have weak hamstrings** because their sports are not recruiting this muscle group enough, unless they are performing a max velocity sprint, and we all know how rarely this occurs. Instead of stretching the hamstrings, come back to the strengthening movements like Deadlifts and Single Leg Deadlifts, as well as work on better mobility in the hip flexors. When the hip flexors are over-activated, the hamstrings take on the pain because the brain goes back into lockdown mode. Beyond strength and mobility work, especially the day after a game, I would rather have a girl go for an easy breezy walk. Please spare her the touching her toes shenanigans. It does nothing.

So, if static stretching is not the answer, then what is? Female athletes are better off focusing on the neurological component of recovery. Meditating pre- and post-game help the nervous system return to a parasympathetic state, so the brain does not go on the defense and lock up the muscles. They are also better off focusing on strength training year-round to make the muscles as durable as possible. **Strength training is also flexibility training.** When a girl performs a Single Leg Deadlift or a Squat through the full range of motion, movements for hamstring and quadricep strengthening, she is lengthening the muscle during the eccentric part of the movement. This alone is enough to work on flexibility, while also bolstering tissue durability, balance, and core stability. Sounds like bang for the buck to me. Static stretching is not the solution for female athletes. They need stronger bodies and calmer minds.

Resetting Posture

If there is one thing a girl can introduce into her recovery regimen, it is focusing on good posture. This is an easy fix that does wonders for proper breathing, parasympathetic nervous system response and mood.

It is a habit that does not waste time or interfere with the daily activities of living, but rather, enhances them. All a girl must do is be mindful of when she is slouching, and to pull herself upright.

Posture plays an important role in performance. As a disclaimer, "perfect posture" is a vague phrase as it will differ for everyone, but there are some things to keep in mind. When a girl is slumped over with her shoulders internally rotated, the weight of her head moves forward, which causes a lower extremity storm. The brain is smart and wants the body in a better position, so it does not fall over. So, what does the brain do? It rolls the pelvis forward, and the hip flexors and knees take on more load. This can decrease stride length for sprinting at max velocity, as well as increase knee pain and instability.

One of the most exciting things about better posture is not just the injury prevention, but the mood enhancement. More research is emerging on the impact of posture on mood, namely, anxiety and depression issues. Looking back on millions of years and how humans evolved, upright posture was how our ancestors were better equipped to interact with the world. It was the determining factor of who won or lost in combat when out hunting. When our ancestors fought animals and beasts, the one who knew he was going to lose and not survive, collapsed his posture. Poor posture is directly linked to these feelings of defeat. This concept, still present in psychology theories today, states that facial expression (i.e., smiling) and open body language influence positive emotion. Collapsed posture has been linked to negative health outcomes such as pain and depression. It also is associated with decline in emotional well-being and energy levels (19). Another study states that adopting an open posture can help to alleviate anxiety (20). One of the most notable studies on posture impact on mood came from a study of 74 participants with the upright participants reporting higher self-esteem, more arousal, and better mood compared to the slumped participants. Slumped participants used more negative emotion words, sadness words, and fewer positive emotion words (21).

I implore all female athletes to try upright posture daily, especially when going for a recovery walk after competition. They will notice their mood and energy come back into equilibrium, and their nasal breathing much easier to execute. Other ways to reset posture:

> Activate the posterior chain (glute bridges)
> Activate the anterior core (nasal breathing)
> Revisit hip flexor mobility (sitting crisscross on floor and standing up with no hands)

The posture of a young female athlete should reflect how she wants to interact with the world, as well as feel. Does she want to show insecurity and feel defeated; or does she want to ooze confidence and feel uplifted the next time she steps back into the competitive arena?

Good posture is only a tiny re-positioning away from immense results.

The Best Injury Reduction Program for Female Athletes

One thing that flabbergasts me is the self-help community. There is not a shortage of books on how to become a better person, live in abundance, and become happier. What gets me though, is the self-help community enables instant gratification. "Read my book to become happier!" or "take my abundance workshop to attract money!" all sound sparkly and amazing, but the folks who read these books and sign up for these courses put in little to no inner work behind closed doors. While people have good intention, they do not follow through on the embodiment. Do not let the people who own crystals and burn sage daily fool you. The people who improve do not just do the superficial work that is broadcasted on social media. Instead, they do the inner work that is hidden behind the scenes. So, how does self-help relate to injury reduction?

The best injury reduction program is not just doing the best movements. The best program is not just having the most advanced technology. The best program is not just doing the exact sets and reps that are outlined. While a well-rounded performance program with proper progression is crucial for youth female athletes, it is just one sliver of the pie. **The best results do not come from the plan alone, but the daily decisions female athletes make in their nutrition, sleep, posture, stress management, and lifestyle.** Many of these decisions are made outside of the training sessions, and in fact, done when no one is watching.

The best program is not the sets and reps of the exercises, but also, the sets and reps done when the coach is not in a female athlete's presence. How many reps per day is she taking a proper nasal breath? How many reps per day is she active? How many reps per day is she walking? How many reps per day is she putting nourishment in her body? How many reps per day is she standing upright and not slouched?

How many reps per day is she off her phone? How many reps per day is she having positive thoughts? How many reps per day is she cheering herself on, rather than criticizing? The female athlete needs to do more than the program. She needs to do more than what is expected and take inventory of all these other components of her life. **A program is as good as the athlete's daily decisions when the coach is not watching.**

The Civilization Crises

Looking at recovery activities like breathing, sleeping, eating, walking, standing upright, and getting off tech, they are becoming harder to execute in the current world. Humanity has steered far, far away from the natural and simple things that have allowed us to evolve for millions of years. We have become stimulated, lazy, anxious, malnourished, sleep deprived, and stressed.

One of my favorite passages from Charles Eisenstein's book, *Sacred Economics,* is a jolting wake-up call:

➢ *We have bigger houses but smaller families;*

➢ *more conveniences, but less time.*

➢ *We have more degrees but less sense;*

➢ *more knowledge but less judgment;*

➢ *more experts, but more problems;*

➢ *more medicines but less healthiness.*

➢ *We've been all the way to the moon and back,*

➢ *but have trouble in crossing the street to meet our new neighbor*

➢ *We built more computers to hold more copies than ever,*

> ➤ *But have less real communication;*
> ➤ *We have become long on quantity,*
> ➤ *but short on quality.*
> ➤ *These are times of fast foods but slow digestion;*
> ➤ *Tall men but short characters;*
> ➤ *Steep profits but shallow relationships.*
> ➤ *It's a time when there is much in the window,*
> ➤ *But nothing in the room.*

This passage presents the comical juxtaposition of our progression with our regression. Technological advancements and progress can make life a walk in the park, but at the same time, make life more sedentary. With more things has also come more injury, sickness, and disease. Have we progressed? Are we truly better off?

In youth female sports, there are more specialists and experts than ever before, but have the ACL numbers improved? There are more teams, elite travel clubs, and skills trainers, but has the overuse and burnout problem been mitigated?

Realizing how convenient life has become, yet how it has played a role in the devolution of humanity, is an important first step to change in female youth sports. In many cases, this is when "going back to the way things were" might be a good thing for young girls. Talented female athletes do not necessarily emerge from fancy performance facilities, more trainers, more gurus, more specialized training, or more shiny gadgets and equipment. They emanate from leaning into the natural simplicities of life that were given to humanity long before technology and complexity were introduced. Female athletes blossom through movement, nourishment, the beauty of nature, and play. They gain strength through loading the body with basic movement patterns. They build confidence by getting off social media and getting to know their souls. This is when the mantra "keep it simple, stupid" serves young female athletes.

Chapter 8: Mental Confidence

"You've got to be confident when you're competing. You've got to be a beast."

– Gabby Douglas

Coaching female athletes has been one of the most rewarding pursuits of my life. What has made me the most over-joyed with my clients has not been the college recruiting and academic success stories. Though those have been impressive accomplishments, I recognize they were the most finite. Many coaches would attribute their career success to how many college or professional athletes they produced, or how many wins and championships they had.

The greatest success I have had as a coach was inspiring girls to love movement, but also to feel confident in their body and mind's strengthening capabilities to handle any adversity in life. Over the years, as my young girls became young women in college, I learned that my role was to give them the power and autonomy to face the world themselves. They no longer needed me to tell them how many sets and reps to do for a Pull-Up. They no longer needed me to cheer them on during grueling conditioning runs. They no longer needed me to motivate them. **The biggest win in my coaching career has been the preparation and development of independent women who can take** charge of their health, and continue to integrate the strength of their bodies and minds for a lifetime.

I have learned that strength training in the gym is the ultimate confidence booster. Putting the body through high amounts of stimulus, adapting and overcoming them to become stronger is downright magical. The gym taught these girls that the body and the mind aren't separate entities, but rather, they are one working in conjunction to overcome high amounts of stimulus. The gym taught these girls that bad days can be turned into amazing days with movement. The gym taught these girls that even when they go through pain, they will become better from it. The gym taught these girls that a breakdown always leads to a breakthrough. After all, girls will continue to go through incredible amounts of duress in their lifetime – whether it's through breakups, losses of loved ones, or career hardships – and they are going to have to find the strength to build themselves up again. Lifting is a metaphor for overcoming trauma – if the muscles can break down, they can build up. If the bones can wane as you age, they can also be made durable again. If the function of the brain can decline, it can also sharpen. The strengthening of the body and mind is a potent tool in the young female athlete's hands for as long as she lives. **Everything lost can be built up again.**

One of the most empowering times in my career was when a young female athlete of mine came into my office and burst into tears. She was going through a plethora of academic, family, and friend issues. Her stress accumulated to a tipping point, and she could not hold it in any longer. I had planned for her to do her Deadlift testing that day, but I figured it wouldn't be the best idea for such a Central Nervous System heavy workout on top of her emotional distress. Instead of giving her the plan, I asked her what she wanted to do. As she sobbed and gasped for air to speak a sentence, she said, "I still want to work out. I know it will make me feel better." As her strength coach, I was shocked that she felt comfortable spilling her guts to me, then proceeding to test her Deadlift max. Nevertheless, it made sense after I pondered a bit: my female athletes are so used to going through insane amounts of duress in my workouts, that testing a Deadlift on a bad day does not faze them. In fact, it empowers them. It was this moment that I realized the impact of exercise on these girls, and its ability to shift their mood and energy in a positive direction. I realized I am not just a strength coach, but an inspiration for living a healthy, empowered life, both mentally and physically.

There have been more inspiring stories, such as the numerous occasions girls came into my facility, and upon initial evaluation, they could not do a single Pull-Up. After several months of training consistently, they were able to bang out not just a bodyweight Pull-Up, but one with added load. They witnessed how malleable the human is, and how it can build incredible strength with consistent effort and commitment to training.

Another favorite has been getting entire families on board with setting up home gyms and the daughters writing the workouts they did "with Coach Erica." I received pictures and videos of everyone crushing it, including the parents and the siblings. I also had girls go off to "Senior Week" in high school, which is known for a week of partying, eating junk, and imbibing alcohol. My girls refused to succumb to the peer pressure, and instead, turned the typical party week into a week of movement and healthy food. Instead of getting pictures of red solo cups and beer pong tables, I received text message with pictures of Acai bowls, smoothies, and beach runs. Darn, I was proud.

I had girls show up to an off-season training session with their own "Fitness Board Game" they created with various challenges, like races, Hang and Push-Up competitions, and Crawling games. Instead of doing the organized session I had planned that day, we played a board game they came up with on their own time without me asking. There were times when sessions were canceled due to inclement weather, and I would still get text messages from my girls with their self-made workout circuits to do on a stormy day.

I can say that each story has its own unique inspiration, but the one that stands out the most was a middle school girl I worked with who took a year off from soccer due to serious health issues. Her doctor recommended a bone marrow transplant (hematopoietic stem cell transplant) because it was the only treatment for her rare diagnoses, aplastic anemia. The transplant process replaces a person's diseased bone marrow with healthy marrow from a donor, and the new marrow goes on to build a healthy blood system. After spending a year in the hospital, she was eager to get back to playing, but it had to be a gradual process to get her acclimated back to full exercise. She came to me with fire in her soul to train because she missed the fulfillment that movement and soccer gave her. Not only was she ready to work out again, but she was ready to pursue her dream of making a higher-level team in her club.

After several months of early morning training sessions with me, she made the top team. For any girl who lost a year of training, this would be extremely challenging. My middle school girl persevered and chipped away slowly at new feats of strength, which resulted in her reaching her goal. This story is a reminder of how capable the mind and body truly are, and I want girls to remember how much magic they have inside them – to empower themselves through movement and a positive mindset.

Confidence As a Muscle

Confidence truly is a muscle.

It does not come from being complacent, nor does it come from expecting it to magically appear. It births from imperfect action, risk taking, stimulating the mind and body, and pushing past the next threshold. Over the years in my coaching career, the one thing that parents always asked of me was to help with their girl's *confidence*. I became flabbergasted that this was a common theme time and time again, and I continued to try to figure out why. I was seeing girls outsource their happiness to others – they were afraid to make mistakes, they were crippled by failure, and they sought approval. This caused them to play it safe on the pitch, and unable to let their inner gems shine. **Confidence, to that end, never comes from staying trapped in one's comfort zone**, and girls need to be encouraged to venture into unknown territory and transcend comfort, so they can see their potential.

One of my favorite coaches was my assistant coach at Johns Hopkins University, who pushed me to take risks to gain confidence in my one-on-one skills. When I worried about making mistakes, he would say to me, "what is the worst that could happen?" Yep, he was right. The world wouldn't end if I lost the ball. My team wouldn't suffer if I lost a one-on-one battle in the attacking third. My value wouldn't decrease as a human if I tried a move and messed up. Ha! It is comical that I even placed my worth on how I performed. **I learned that it was a greater cost not to try and see what was on the other side of comfort.** As I took more risks and took on more defenders, tried more dazzling moves, and maneuvered around my opponents, I realized that I was capable. It was like magic. Having my coach believe in me and encourage me to put aside my failure of messing up and be bold with my skills, was what I needed to gain confidence.

Confidence is a muscle. It is not developed from a single session with a private trainer. It is not elevated by one day of journaling. It is not improved by watching a motivational video. It becomes unshakeable when girls see it as a lifetime pursuit. Just like strengthening the hips, the core, and the upper body, female athletes need to commit to confidence training daily. Their coaches can push them, but then the onus is on the female athletes to build their confidence muscle. Sure, I can give my girls all the positive affirmations and words of encouragement as a coach, but if they are going home and bringing themselves down and resorting to toxic mental habits, or not taking risks at training sessions, I become useless. While I love reminding girls of their strengths, it is dangerous for them to outsource their confidence levels to me   to rely on me to save them. This takes them out of their power, and the constant seeking of approval and happiness from others.

I do not want girls to depend on others for their own happiness and fulfilment, nor do I want them to feel happy only after a check-in call with me. Rather, I want them to find happiness in themselves. True confidence building happens when girls are relentlessly consistent with:

- Participating in positive self-talk
- Journaling their strengths and skills (are they fast, strong, aggressive, creative, skilled?)
- Writing a list of what they offer the world besides their sport talents (are they good teammates, good friends, motivating to others, kind?)
- Being mindful of when they are comparing and being jealous, but shifting the focus back on the themselves
- Doing things that bring them joy (leisure, less social media, time with friends)
- Surrounding themselves with friends who support their mission
- Getting rid of the drama and gossip friend group that is wearing them down
- Meditating or spending time to be silent
- Taking risks at practices
- Leaning into discomfort
- Being okay with failing a lot
- Taking action to learn from their failures

Coaches are not the panacea to a female athlete's confidence issues; they are just facilitators. The female athlete needs to take charge of her mental training; train it like a muscle, and have an insatiable desire to do so. She must lean into discomfort and expose herself to environments that raise her confidence threshold.

I have had to do this in sports and in my lifetime – the building of confidence never stops, so girls need to prepare now. The summer before I played at Johns Hopkins University, I played pick-up with the boys several times a week to get more confident with my skills under pressure and speed, as well as boost my creativity. Though it was out of my comfort zone to play with the boys, it pushed me to become a more confident player, and when I went to college for pre-season, I won every one-on-one drill and earned a starting spot freshman year.

The confidence journey has not stopped in the real world either. As a working woman, I've had to gain confidence in my coaching skills by diving into the unknown and downright uncomfortable. The first time I worked with a large group of athletes was at a large performance facility with a group of 40 high school lacrosse players. Prior to this, I was doing smaller one-on-one sessions and had no experience overseeing a big group. On the first day of work, I was flustered and overwhelmed from the mayhem. The second day, I got better at organizing the group and making the workout efficient. The third, fourth, and fifth days, I knew how to command a room of young athletes and demand respect. Now, coaching large groups is one of my favorite things; in fact, I am energized by it. My confidence blossomed because I went headfirst into an anxiety inducing situation. Had I not tried working with so many athletes, I would never have discovered that my true love is coaching large groups of athletes. Moreover, I would not have been able to impact thousands of players if I had played it safe with one-on-one sessions.

Even with leisure activities, confidence needs to be trained. When I learned snowboarding for the first time, it was the ultimate test of building confidence – from the endless falling and crashing into trees on the trail – with each time I got a little bit better. Did it totally suck in the beginning? Yes. Did I throw tantrums and cry and wallow in self-pity and frustration? Absolutely. Was I the most miserable person to be with on the slopes? You bet. My friend who taught me deserves credit for dealing with my frustrated self, but I am so grateful he was there to guide me. After each fall, I learned a new way to control my speed. After each tree crash, I learned a new way to maneuver my feet on the board. After learning to control my speed and maneuver, I then progressed to going down more difficult, steeper trails. After tackling more challenging trails, I went on to jumps. As my confidence grew, I took more risks. Now, I am grateful I pushed past the discomfort to become an advanced snowboarder, and it has become my favorite activity, second to soccer. It brings me so much joy.

Everyone needs to get an itty bit more uncomfortable each step of the way. It's worth it.

Becoming More Aggressive

One of the most popular questions I have been asked during my coaching career has been, "how do I get my daughter to be more aggressive?" Oftentimes, parents get frustrated when their daughter lacks that extra spark during competition and wonder if it can even be trained. Spoiler: yes, it can. However, aggression is not developed by girls doing skills sessions that have minimal to zero defensive pressure, nor is it developed by yelling, "be more aggressive!" No amount of screaming at female athletes to play harder will suffice. No amount of hiring extra trainers will help either, unless they have a deep understanding of child development.

So, how do young girls develop tenacity? All it takes is confidence and female athletes must immerse themselves in uncomfortable environments that are not their sport practices and games. Developing confidence comes from being uncomfortable, and being forced to navigate challenging scenarios using their physicality. If we want the adaptation of improved aggressive play, then the stimulus must be greater and more intense than what they are experiencing in an organized setting. Remember in the beginning chapters, I discussed how my brother and I used to wrestle? It is an environment such as this that is needed. **Girls need to stop being bubble wrapped from situations that call for physical contact. I mean come on, do people think they will bolt into a tackle at high velocities if they have not been exposed to a tougher environment?** The fact that I was familiar with being physical with my brother made tackles in my soccer games incredibly easy. Physical contact in soccer did not phase me.

To get even more confident in my physical ability, I also resistance trained and strengthened my body. This gave me an incredible amount of confidence to handle being physical in the game, and not being reluctant to push around the bigger girls. I was far, far from a feeble player. Therefore, the winning line-up for developing aggressive female athletes is this:

1. **Resistance Training**

2. **Rough Free Play (wrestling, grappling, shielding)**

It is the integration of these two components that will turn girls into warriors. The resistance training is the organized setting needed to progress a girl, so she executes safe technique and builds stronger muscles. In contrast, the rough free play is the unstructured, unsupervised setting needed to expose her to an environment at a higher intensity than her sport, and bolster her ability to navigate unpredictable stimuli.

That's it. That's all they need. Aggression does not need to be overcomplicated. So long as female athletes master these two year-round, they will blossom into aggressive athletes who embrace physical contact. If these are not done and parents are still complaining that their girl is not aggressive, I do not know what to say except it is their fault for failing their female athletes.

Perfectionism Is a Myth

Chasing perfection is a losing game.

It can leave the female athlete feeling discouraged and flat. It is a pursuit that becomes an unending cycle of frustration. Striving to be perfect goes against the human condition, as well as the nature of life. It is hard to go through sports without mistakes. It is hard to go through life without failure. What matters most is, how these adversities are handled. Psychologist, Tal Ben-Shahar, an authority figure in the field of Positive Psychology, discusses in his work the differences between a perfectionist and "optimalist." The perfectionist uses failure as a definition of their self-worth, and most of the time, they end up giving up. In the other corner, an optimalist uses failure as the impetus to adapt and level up.

A lot of young girls are afraid to make mistakes, and I totally get it because they want to fit in, prove themselves, and make their coaches and parents proud. However, they need to be rooted in reality: mistakes are inevitable. They are going to happen as long as a girl is in sport and living on planet Earth. Perfectionism is a myth, and I learned this at a young age when I dribbled to my team's goal and scored an own goal at age 6. I learned this in high school when I missed a State Cup final penalty kick. I learned this in college when I missed a Conference final penalty kick. Mistakes aren't exclusive to young female athletes. Even at the highest level, professionals make mistakes, too. Lionel Messi has missed penalty kicks. Alex Morgan did not finish every goal scoring opportunity in the box. Kobe Bryant did not make every free throw. **There is solace in knowing that perfectionism is indeed a myth, and no one can make it through sports with a clean slate.** All girls are going to make mistakes, face challenges, and have a handful of "oh crap!" moments. It's the nature of the game.

When it comes to overcoming the perfectionist trap, I look to Stoic philosophy. "A gem cannot be polished without friction, nor a man perfected without trials," Seneca says. Like these raw stones, we need friction to become our best. Achieving success means girls must fully immerse themselves in a storm of highs and lows because success is never linear. Straight lines are boring, aren't they? If girls are going through life turning, curving, falling, rising, oscillating, they are doing themselves a service. Mistakes are the learning curves to greater accomplishment, and when big dreams are achieved, it makes the mistakes worth it.

What kills me about perfectionism is it stagnates female athletes because they are so frozen with being incorrect that they do not act. Imagine a world if everyone waited for the right moment; no risks would be taken. As a result, sports would lack color and vibrancy because no one would ever try to take on a defender, try a sparkling move, go in for a tough tackle, or rocket that shot from half field. With these risks, mistakes will happen, and that is okay. What blocks female athletes from taking risks is the chance of a negative outcome and the shame that comes with making a mistake. The truth is, the consequences of taking risks are inevitable. The pain of failing is what holds girls back and traps them in their perfectionist ways, unaware of their limitless potential. Everyone wants to go through life pain free and avoid suffering at all costs. The pain, however, is a part of sport and life, so the question is, what do female athletes' value that is worth fighting for and experiencing a bit of pain?

There must be something so meaningful to them, like getting better in their sport, becoming their strongest selves, or boosting speed, that they must be okay with the hard work and grit that come with all of this. I am not going to massage this concept and make everyone feel all warm and fuzzy on the inside; rather, failure is a part of the experience of working toward something meaningful, and if a female athlete wants the benefits of improved performance, she must live with the costs, too. There is no bubble wrapping of girls to protect them from the consequences of taking risks in sports; otherwise, if they do not take a leap of faith, they will become complacent and stagnant. They must want to invest the time, push through hard trainings, overcome high stimulus in the gym, and accept the pain when they fail. Sports and life are all about cost-benefit analysis, and girls will continue this in business, their career, and relationships for a lifetime. With any relationship, they will have to accept the emotional volatility, the incredible adventures, the tough disagreements, the negotiations, and feelings of love and joy. With any business venture, they will have to accept the risk of investing and the tremendous return. With any medical career, they will have to accept the long hours in the hospital and feelings of fulfilment of saving lives. The costs are significant in any pursuit, but are they worth it enough to experience the elating benefits?

On the brighter side, the discouragement associated with cost is so fleeting that it only lasts for a split second or a few minutes. Just like clouds in the sky, or a drizzle, or a tumultuous hurricane, it comes and goes. To put things into perspective, minor setbacks are so trivial as humans spin around on planet Earth in the middle of a vast galaxy. They're just a blip in time.

Psychologist Carol Dweck speaks about the "Growth Mindset" as a tool for people to use when emotional pain from failures does happen. People with a growth mindset see failure as an opportunity to learn, view criticism as constructive, see taking risks and trying new things as tools for building competence and confidence, and determine their abilities by their effort and attitude. Mistakes need to be embraced. That is when the creativity is birthed. Furthermore, **overcoming one mistake at a time raises a female athlete's confidence threshold, and she gains more and more confidence each time she gets a reward from her risk.**

The best thing a female athlete can do is to keep the momentum going, learn along the way, and gain confidence through the tough times. When everything is going smooth, no lessons are birthed, and we remain in our comfort zones. But when times get rocky, that's when the female athlete sharpens her craft. "Take those chances and you can achieve greatness, whereas if you go conservative, you'll never know. I truly believe what doesn't kill you makes you stronger. Even if you fail, learning and moving on is sometimes the best thing," race car driver, Danica Patrick beautifully said.

A female athlete needs to abandon perfectionism. She needs to be courageous, not give up, take risks, and lean into uncertainty. Worst case, it does not work out, but hey, the effort is worth it. When things do go her way (and they will!) it is a delightful confidence boost. Stop chasing perfection and start gaining momentum.

Lean into Risk

By signing this waiver you agree to the death risk associated with your skydive experience.

This was an agreement for me I had to sign when I tried skydiving for the first time.

I signed the waiver. I signed, knowing my life was on the line. I signed fully aware of my mortality. I signed understanding that jumping out of a plane was dangerous. I signed because I chose an adrenaline-infused, outrageous and thrilling experience. This was not the only time I have plunged into danger – fearless, bold and excited. I slept in the Amazon jungle with tarantulas bigger than my head, poisonous snakes, and deadly mosquitoes, with no protection and nothing but a hammock. I ate maggots. I canoed in anaconda infested waters. I hang glided over Rio de Janeiro, with nothing but a t-shirt and soccer shorts on, strapped to a total stranger. I hiked Machu Picchu, ate chickens for dinner, and slept in a precarious native hut with critters crawling on me during my slumber. I've zip-lined upside down, knowing my helmet wouldn't save me from the 2,000-foot fall. I've snowboarded at 11,000 feet, shredded through forests, rocketed off jumps, and zipped down Double Black Diamond trails. I chose all these activities, fully understanding I might get bit by a snake, might free fall from the sky, might break some bones, might get eaten alive, might get a concussion from hitting a tree, and might break my spine from not landing a jump. All things considered, **I threw myself into some dangerous and breathtaking moments because I longed to experience the fullness of life – to explore uncharted territory, encounter new creatures and wildlife, push my body to challenging physical limits, expand my mental capacity, and adapt to unfamiliar environments.** Not only did I crave adventure, but I threw myself into it because I felt prepared – physically, mentally, and emotionally. I trusted myself, as a malleable human, to be able to mold to my surroundings, adapt, and become more resilient.

159

All human begins on planet Earth approach risk at every corner; in fact, they become intimate with it; anxious of their mortality, yet continuing with their lives because they know they are capable. Hopefully, everyone understands risk is an inevitable facet of life, and it is impossible to avoid at all costs. To long for life to be secure, safe and certain, is to ignore its oscillating essence. To want guarantee of stability is to be dead, not alive. It is to ignore being the most wholehearted expression of oneself – a creative, multi-dimensional being here to adapt, overcome and thrive. Some long for order and stability, while ignoring the chaos and uncertainty that makes up the Earth.

What would a life look like if secure? What would a life look like if played safe? What would a life look like if we didn't dive into novelty? I'm noticing that there is less free play, less risk taking, less liberation, less problem solving, and more fear, more safeguarding, more walking on eggshells, more fear of making mistakes, and more bubble wrapping.

Why is it that I hear parents afraid to send their kids into the neighborhood to play with friends? Why is it that I hear coaches shying away from tackle and roughhousing drills? Why is it that when a young girl loses a competition, we solace her and express pity? Why is that when a girl gets defeated and throws a crying fit, her parents rush to comfort her? Why is that everyone receives a trophy even though they lost? Sports are the ultimate risk - everyone gets knocked down, loses, fights back, loses again and again. Stability and safety are never guaranteed in sports, so why are we not encouraging risk taking on the field and off? Why are we fear mongering so much?

Why aren't we, instead, encouraging female athletes to prepare, to get strong, to embrace their capacity to adapt, to challenge themselves, to lean into struggle? Why aren't we exposing them to various environments that challenge human potential? They might fall? They might scrape a knee? They might get a boo-boo? By stepping onto the field, young female athletes risk all of this – rolling an ankle, tearing an ACL, getting a concussion, bruising a quad, or breaking an arm. We cannot erase risk, otherwise we would not be playing the beautiful, dynamic game. We cannot go for every tackle, every one-on-one battle, every air ball, every contact with reluctance and self-doubt. How would the magic happen? How would we try new things? How would we know what we're capable of physically, technically and tactically? How competitive would sports be? How fulfilled would young female athletes feel? How creative would they be? Would sports exist?

I am so passionate about teaching young girls about fearlessness, risk taking, and confidence because fear holds them back from showing their true colors, pursuing their passions, and living their purpose. Fear is the ultimate robber of creativity and confidence. Without coming face to face with fear, and overcoming it, confidence cannot rise. Creativity cannot flourish. If girls remain in the same comfort zone of going through the motions, they will never be aware of their potential on the other side.

Instead, why don't we use fear as an impetus for action? We can make it less intimidating if we prepare and put in the work year-round, and for a lifetime. In fact, we can go the extra mile so that our body is resilient and robust. When we step onto the pitch, we do not second guess, we do not overthink, we do not hesitate, but simply, we create, we fight, we compete, and we do not bat an eye. We play with confidence and conviction – going into slide tackles, jumping for air balls, nudging and shielding defenders, and bolting down the field at speed with grace and poise. If we tiptoed around playing our hardest due to the fear of getting hurt, messing up, or letting down the squad, we would not be optimizing our potential, and we should not be playing sports. We would not be leaning into what makes us spontaneous, beautiful, exuberant and dramatic.

What would the girls' sports world be if we exclaimed, "do not tackle that player, you might hurt her!" or "do not go for that air ball, you might roll an ankle when you land!" or "do not wrestle with your friends, you might get bruised!"

What are the daily habits put in for a lifetime to be ready for when the going gets tough? I will say this: things will prove a lot harder than ankle rolls one day. A forceful tackle. A head collision. A sharper change of direction. A final sprint in overtime. A board meeting at a company. The MCAT for medical school. A TEDx talk. An interview. A presentation. A business investment. A divorce. A job lay-off. Are girls strong in their mind, body and soul to not just face these hurdles, but to leap over them with confidence?

It is all the same message: **we do our best to prepare so we can be more confident, and at peace with risk taking.**

What is a life without risk? Nothing at all. As Eastern philosopher Osho states, "death is secure. Life is insecurity. One who really wants to live has to live in danger, in constant danger. One wants to reach to the peaks has to take the risk of getting lost. One who wants to climb the highest peaks has to take the risk of falling from somewhere, slipping down." It is not about deleting risks, but it is more about making them an itty bit less scary by doing the daily work to be prepared.

Do we continue meandering down the path of not taking risks, at the expense of not living? Do we teach our girls to hide, to stare at glowing screens, to become entranced by social media, to outsource their happiness, and to ignore their strengths? Should we not allow them to adventure and to explore? On the other hand, do we continue to teach them to be humans, who were put on this planet to invite risk? To adapt. To overcome challenges. To survive sickness. To get stronger through sports. To evolve from adversity. To make it out of tackles. To level up. To attack pull-up bars with weight strapped on.

This is resilient science – a science that cannot be measured by health statistics and 'experts.' It does not have data points, trends, graphs, or numbers. How can it? How can we measure something that infuses us with joy?

How can we measure the fulfillment we get from training hard and lasting a 90-minute match? How can we measure the accomplishment we feel after coming back stronger from an injury? How can we measure the smile we have when we get our first chained pull-up?

I cannot measure a colorful life through a research study.

I cannot measure trekking through Peru for four days and making it to the top of Machu Picchu. I cannot measure the adrenaline rush that comes from jumping out of a plane. I cannot measure the pleasure from getting lost on an island for three hours and finding paradise. I cannot measure the thrill a human gets from hiking the Amazon jungle and catching piranhas for dinner. I cannot measure the gratification that comes from training for years and getting through the uncomfortable reps and becoming a two-time All-American. I cannot measure the sense of accomplishment a young athlete gets from trying a sparkling move against a defender and leaving them in the dust. I cannot measure the joy of a kid who knocked an opponent off the ball in double overtime to score the winning goal. I cannot measure the beaming smile of a young athlete and the fullness of her heart when she risks breaking her back, yet she scores off of a bicycle kick. I cannot measure the empowerment a woman gets from surviving an abusive relationship and escaping from mental brainwash.

I cannot measure any of this, and had I not taken any risks in my life, I would have not traveled the world, met amazing beings, played soccer abroad, coached kids in Brazil, seen the lush Amazon Rainforest, realized my physical potential, reached my peak as a college soccer player, started a business, or wrote this book.

If your life only centers around the quantifiable things, the peer-reviewed science, and the measurements, you are in the wrong place. If you are here for the health data analysis, leave now. If you are here to grasp resilient science with numbers, do not bother. Humans are too dynamic, too unique to be narrowed down to data points, measured by numbers, and defined by charts. We do not follow science. Science follows us. And it better keep up.

I want to hammer home that fear lurks at every turn – youth sports, career, disease, academics, travel, every industry, every pursuit, every action, every step, every investment, every hobby, everything.

We never say:

"Don't make that investment, you'll lose money."

"Don't be the first to climb Mount Everest, you'll die."

Or, "don't start that business, you'll go into debt."

Or, "don't get married, you might get divorced."

Or, "don't get that TEDx talk, you'll get hate."

Or, "don't snowboard, you might break a leg."

Or, "don't play your sport. You'll get hurt."

Or, "don't hug someone. You might get sick."

The risks from all of these – career, sports, viruses – aren't as terrifying if people educate themselves, believe in themselves, and do the work by preparing to the best of their ability. If a female athlete consistently puts in thousands of hours of strengthening, preparing, building and adapting, and bolstering her immune system through good training and lifestyle habits, they are less likely to get injured, be sick, and suffer.

It takes work, though.

It is freaking hard to take inventory of one's life, so incredibly hard. I would be a terrible mentor to female athletes if I did not encourage them to challenge themselves, overcome feats of strength, be creative, try new moves, go for that starting position, go up in weight on the dead lift, push through that extra sprint, try a bicycle kick, attempt a flip throw-in, lean into risk, and adapt.

What path are we heading down if we safeguard at all costs, and allow future generations to stagnate? What type of young athlete are we shaping? One who is a fearful clone of society? One who sees life as a predator to be avoided?

Or...

One who sees life as an adventure to be lived?

Lean into risk.

Comparison and Jealousy are Unproductive

I was bullied a lot as a teenage athlete.

At the time, I was on a travel soccer team, and was the player who scored the most, played the most minutes, and got the most recognition. Alas, with great stats and performance, comes great envy and hate. There was one teammate who bullied me and said things like "you think you're hot sh*t," "you're not that good," "you're just the coach's favorite," and "you don't deserve to start over me." With this narrative, she berated my hard work and talents so that she could feel good about herself. The bullying went on for several months, and while there were glimpses of feeling defeated by her comments, I decided to take the high road, the most positive course of action, and continue to do what made me successful: focus on myself.

When other girls hate, that means they have something inside themselves that they are insecure about. **If someone is jealous, it most likely is an attempt to cover up their own shortcomings and weaknesses.** Anytime a teammate is jealous, and a female athlete gives it attention, she takes away her own power. I urge girls to focus on what they can control: their habits, their training, and their self-improvement. There are so many moving pieces to improved performance – training, nutrition, sleep, breath work, daily movement and so much more – that any time a female athlete gives a hater attention, she takes away from one or more of these pieces. Time is limited, so girls need to get clear on where they spend it. In fact, **girls need to see their minds as a high value asset and protect it at all costs. They need to say no to the noise, no to the drama, and no to the hate.** It is much more liberating to do so.

During my college career, I had to refocus back to myself constantly. Being on a team with a roster of 35 was immensely competitive, and each year I refused to give up my starting spot and playing time. After my freshman season, I remember our head coach sending out a list of the incoming freshmen – where they were from, what amazing club team they were on, and all their high school accolades. Sure, I was nervous as new, talented freshmen entered the program, but I used those nerves as fuel train hard in the off-season. I could have been jealous by their accolades and shaking in my boots, but that energy was better spent working to improve who I was.

I urge female athletes to tackle jealousy and comparison with bringing the focus back to themselves. They must focus on mastering their craft first, because it's far more productive. A female athlete cannot be her best version when she is looking outside of herself, comparing to others, and expressing jealousy toward her peers. As clinical psychologist Jordan Peterson says, "set your house in perfect order before you criticize the world."

Defining Self Worth

I often ask my female athletes: "who are you?"

Many are floored by this question because it forces them to go within the depths of their souls and discover who they are beyond the athlete label. When I ask, "who are you?" there are girls who give the clueless "I don't know" answer. Truth is, no one knows who they really are because they are distracted by their external reality – scrolling social media, comparing to others, and outsourcing their worth to titles, achievements, and accolades. When they score a goal, they feel better about themselves. When they ace a test, they are finally happy. When they get that starting position, they are no longer depressed. When they get a compliment, they are no longer insecure. When they get that scholarship, they are no longer unfulfilled. Defining self-worth by what they accomplish causes them to fluctuate through an endless swirl of extreme emotions – from intoxicating highs, to deflating lows. Too many girls define their self-worth by their ability to play their sport, the club team they are on, the minutes they play, the team that recruits them, or the goals they score. Although these are important accomplishments, young female athletes are worth more than all these superficial, fleeting moments.

It is important for them to explore what else they offer because one day, they must face the reality of their sport ending. I do not want them to have an identity crisis because they were one-dimensional for their entire life and have no other passions and talents on which to fall back. Female athletes should look inside themselves and ask what truly defines their worth. Are they good listeners when their friends are down? Are they the inspiration to others to live a healthy life? Are they the jovial ones who can make their entire friend group belly laugh? Are they at peace with themselves when they are alone? Are they after a greater purpose to serve the younger generations that follow them? **Character, morals, and purpose matter far more than accolades, statistics, and grades.**

Be a Victor

Life is difficult.

At a minimum, girls will experience a series of challenges and will need to be equipped to handle these with courage. A female athlete who is truly resilient stands in the face of fear, and is fully confident in her ability to prevail. **She tackles failure with full self-responsibility and grace, rather than blame and victimhood.**

Admittedly, I am sick of the victim mindset amongst females. It oozes into a girl's psyche at a young age from pop culture, celebrities, social media, and women in the professional world, and I am over it. I am over girls playing small. I am tired of girls playing victims. I am exhausted from girls blaming the outcome of their lives on others. I am tired of girls saying they do not have opportunity. This happens a lot because it is easy to blame rather than take responsibility and see where one fell short. It is easy to yell at a goalkeeper, when a female athlete did not help defend on the same play. It is easy to blame the coach for lack of playing time, when a female athlete did not work hard enough. It is easy to blame a college coach for not recognizing talent, when a female athlete did not do anything to stand out above the noise.

Blaming and playing the victim is a losing game and it takes girls out of their power. If they adopt this mindset in youth sport, then how much will it permeate into their adult life? Will they blame colleagues for them not being able to get a promotion? Will they blame their boss for not getting paid enough? In any situation, there is always a choice to be the victim or the victor. The victor is guided by self-responsibility and their work ethic. If they are not getting enough playing time, is it because they are not working hard enough? Are they staying on the wrong team where they are not respected? It is the girl's choice to act and change the situation. In the workplace, if they are not getting paid enough, is it because they are not going above and beyond? Is it because they have not spoken to their boss and made a case for a higher salary? Is it because they chose a low-paying job? Do they need to shift companies or careers? In dating, is a girl in a bad relationship because it is the boyfriend's fault, or is she not being clear on how she wants to be treated? There is always a part of the story where oneself is at fault for staying stuck in crappy situations.

Take being a female coach in a male dominated industry. Oh, hi! That is me. I could easily blame the patriarchy for my lack of opportunity, but instead, I make active choices to work hard, master my craft more every year, have the confidence to ask for promotions, and know when to set clear boundaries. Since these mindset shifts, I've excelled in a male dominated industry, live in more abundance, and am given far more opportunities than my male colleagues. I want to be the inspiration for young girls because I do not complain. I take action.

Be a victor. Not a victim.

Owning Your Strengths and Accomplishments

It is okay for female athletes to showcase, let alone, be proud of their strengths. There is too much fit-, health-, and talent-shaming going on, but this comes from people who are insecure. I want female athletes who are fit and talented to realize that the haters are going to hate, and the girls will have to deal with naysayers. Doing something bold and amazing always comes with a side of criticism. Author Mark Manson states it beautifully, "you cannot be a powerful and life-changing presence to some people without being a joke or an embarrassment to others." During my college playing career, I evolved by making a drastic shift in my nutrition and training regimen for the better. While my friends gobbled down greasy food and sugary sports drinks, I fueled with veggies and protein.

Let me be honest for a second: I succumbed to the Freshman 15. I'd be lying if I said it wasn't true, but yes, many college athletes are easily sucked into the pizza buffets and dessert displays at the campus cafeteria. Added to that is the weight gain from booze consuming alcohol. It is an issue, as there is peer pressure, binge drinking, and parties. I'm not going to tip toe around the issue and act like college is all rainbows, book clubs, and study groups.

As I began to tweak my nutrition in a way that supported my physical performance as well as cognitive function, I never turned back. My playing reached amazing heights, my creativity flourished, and my speed and explosiveness left opponents in the dust.

In all fairness, I should be able to talk about my growth and accomplishments without being called a "bragger." Leading scorer every season, broke midfielder scoring records, National Midfielder of the Year, Conference Player of the Year, Academic All-American, Dean's List, Scholar All-American, and the list goes on. There are many layers as to why I hid my tail between my legs and let my mom speak when people asked about the glowing successes in my career – societal norms, personal insecurity, fit-shaming, and fear of what others would say. I believe women are discouraged from growing and building and blossoming and celebrating how amazing they are. As an example, when I started to eat healthier, take care of my body, and dial in to all aspects of my performance, such as sleep, stress management, academics, friendships, a lot of my friends would say to me, "you've changed" or "you're getting a salad?!" Was this them genuinely concerned for me? Or was it the other girls remaining stagnant themselves, not taking responsibility for their lives, and shaming me for the power moves I was making?

I believe the latter.

Nowadays, fit-shaming is just as dangerous as fat-shaming.

Do not get me wrong, fat-shaming is bad, and we should not police others for what they choose to put into their bodies. So let me leave it at this: no matter what others do, whether they choose to consume nutrients or toxic junk, the shaming needs to stop. Maybe I will change the world posting my big salads stacked with copious amounts of protein, fish and meat on Instagram. Maybe I will not. But it is not my burden to change others' behaviors, nor is it my job to expect others to be like me.

All I can do, and all female athletes can do, is lead by example and inspire. That's it.

Be The Inspiration

I urge female athletes who are dedicated to their training, nutrition and everything that keeps them healthy, to keep the momentum going. The world needs more inspiration from those pouring love into themselves.

We live in a world where fit people are seen as privileged. We live in a world where talking about natural medicine is censored. We live in a world where doctors discussing movement and sunlight are called quacks. We live in a world where healthy people are called "conspiracy theorists." We live in a world where women's muscles are not celebrated enough. We live in a world where meditating and taking a break from social media isn't normal. We live in a world where eating healthy is seen as restrictive.

Some days, I feel like I'm in the twilight zone – that fit-shaming is the norm of the future, and it's toxic to inspire others with your health and well-being. "You're privileged. You're spoiled," they screech to me.

Just like all humans, I have been exposed to empowering, healthy information as much as I have been exposed to demeaning and toxic information. I have been exposed to drugs. I have been exposed to alcohol. I have been exposed to tobacco propaganda. I have been exposed to abusive relationships. I have been exposed to McDonald's, foods high in oils and bad fats. I have been exposed to downright unhealthy living. It is splattered everywhere. Everyone is exposed to both ends. **Amidst all the sickness and temptations in society, is it a privilege that I actively chose not to participate in these, and instead, live a healthy and fit life?** Is it a privilege I work hard day in and day out to be my healthiest self? Is it a privilege no one saved me, but myself?

Yes, I went to one of the best public-school systems in the country, but did I learn anything about health, preventative medicine, cognition function, and food as healing? Not at all. I taught myself. I researched. I connected. I talked to others. I dug for information. I embraced nature. I studied natural law. I listened to my body's needs. None of this was learned in a textbook, nor was it dependent on how much money I had in the bank. I just went out to explore and did what my soul was telling me. **I created my privilege.**

I found that the richest people, were in fact, the unhealthiest. Over-consuming. Over-stimulating. Over-buying. Over-eating. Over-stressing. **Returning to simplicity and embracing a minimalist life**

was what liberated me from a profoundly ill society. When I lived in the Amazon jungle with nothing but a fishing hook, a hammock, a machete, and a canoe, I was my happiest and healthiest. It confuses me when people say healthy folks are rich and privileged, when most are out in nature eating natural foods, and they're away from the GMOs, pills, television sets, screens, and the immune suppressing indoors. My biggest light bulb moment occurred when I realized that the health practices I do are free – free sunlight, free movement and walking, free rest, and free meditation. I will continue to be loud with my message to spread information to the world. For free.

Alas, people still fit-shame those spreading empowering information.

It is tough to leave the shackles of a society that imprisons girls to play the victim. If people opt for this, it is not my responsibility to bully people for their decisions, but I beg, don't shame me for my way of living, calling it a privilege. **This is hard freaking work - to say no to life's temptations and addictions.** So, for female athletes who are healthy, and are totally rocking it in their diet and lifestyle, I say screw the noise and own it. Do not let others gaslight you by saying you are spoiled or privileged because you are making a healthy active choice, let alone, implementing thousands of positive habits day in and day out when you could easily plop on a couch and not work toward your dreams.

If anything, female athletes can be the inspiration in a world of misinformation. If anything, female athletes can be the hope in a world of despair. If anything, female athletes can be the warriors in a world of bullies. If anything, female athletes can be the victors in a world of victims.

Taking Inventory and Action

The best way to move into a victor mindset, is to take inventory of one's life. The first step for female athletes to live empowered lives is to cultivate deep self-awareness and get familiar with personal shortcomings and weaknesses. Though it is scary and downright stomach knotting to come face to face with their imperfections, it is the only way to move toward the light. Too many girls are overstimulated, over distracted, and overtrained. It is no wonder they fail to recover, take care of their bodies, and calm their minds. They are so out of touch with how they are feeling and what they need. They refuse to sit down and take inventory of their lives because it births feelings of discomfort and shame. Instead of doing the tough self-evaluation in silence, they resort to the noise - the pills, the quick fixes, the ice bags, the dopamine hits, the rapid pleasures, and the glowing screens. As a result, they ignore their underlying issues that have been keeping them trapped for a long time.

Though it feels icky at first, self-evaluation is what sets female athletes free. They can use it as a tool for a lifetime when they work in high performance jobs, become wives, and mothers. I always tell my athletes, "Health is wealth." Being in good physical and mental health allows girls to live more purposeful, meaningful, joyful, and adventure-filled lives. I compiled an inventory list called "The 7 Gems" of lifestyle components that affect both mental and physical health. I evaluate these daily, and this practice has changed my life. I implore all female athletes to utilize this list weekly to see where they are thriving and where they are lacking:

1. Purpose

2. Relationships

3. Nutrition

4. Physical Health

5. Mental Health

6. Sleep

7. Leisure

Gem #1: Purpose

"What is the meaning of life?"

This was the first question on my Buddhism exam at Johns Hopkins University. It's a deep question that jolted my entire being and left me staring at the classroom ceiling in disbelief. I struggled for an answer.

'What IS the meaning of life?' I asked myself as I twirled my pen in between my fingers. I felt uneasy. I was worried about how to articulate my answer because of nervousness over my final grade. My graduating GPA depended on my ability to give a meaningful answer to this question. Truthfully, I could not tell if I was anxious about my grade, the big question, or both. I took a deep breath as I leaned back in my chair, closed my eyes, and moved into a mini meditation. Our professor taught us to meditate when searching for an answer. As I focused on my breathing, I swam through the depths of my consciousness. Within a few minutes, an answer birthed from my being.

The meaning of life is to accept suffering, but not be attached to it, nor defined by it. Humans are here to find joy in the richness of life – the ups, downs, twists, turns, highs and lows - and to pursue their highest purpose, to serve themselves and cultivate the healthiest version of them, so they can serve their community and inspire younger generations. It means fighting for what is meaningful to them and uplifts all of humanity through health, happiness and purpose. The meaning of life is to define your purpose and use it for the good of others.

That was my answer to the question on my Buddhism final exam. That was the answer that oozed out of my heart. That was the answer that felt genuine. I still stand by this answer today in my coaching career in female sports, and in my human experience in life. Everything I do today – taking care of my health, staying strong, eating well – is all for serving youth and inspiring their future. I am intentional with how I live my life because I know young girls are observing and trying to emulate everything I do.

Finding purpose is the foundation to human existence, and it is the backbone to serving oneself as well as the community. It is the most crucial gem, and the other gems cannot function without it. **Purpose is the meaning attached to one's sport and life, and is what lights a fire within the soul to keep going, even when things get difficult.** I cannot tell anyone what their purpose should be, as it is unique to one's emotions. The first question to ask is this: "why am I playing my sport?"

178

I have asked this numerous times to my female athletes, and they give me answers like "it is fun," "it is something to do," or "it is good to be around friends." While these reasons are a great start, they're not enough. **Deeper emotions need to be attached to the pursuit of one's sport, and it is this meaning that guides girls through challenging times.**

Sports should make girls feel a certain way – feel alive, powerful, present, joyful, strong, carefree, creative, liberated, and vibrant. Whatever the feeling is, it must be what keeps everyone plowing through and consistent in their pursuits because the benefits outweigh the costs. The feelings of elation outweigh the feelings of defeat. The same goes for the other gems, like nutrition, for example. Reasons such as losing weight or looking good aren't enough to have a sustainable nutrition or training plan. Rather, "I feel lethargic and slow, and not confident in myself when I am overweight" is more like it. The feeling attached to the goal gives more significance and value. Humans thrive when they have a positive purpose that keeps the momentum going in sport and in life. They fight for what ignites their soul to be their best version.

Soccer was immensely meaningful to me as a young female athlete, and it saved me from heading down a dark path. When I was in high school, I was a victim of physical and emotional abuse, and there were days when I was so drained, that I struggled to stay afloat and muster up the energy to get out of bed. **Soccer, however, was the most meaningful activity in my life that was worth waking up for, and it was my escape during this time.** When I was playing soccer, I felt alive and vibrant, and I was fully immersed in my creative state. When I was

179

training and lifting weights, I had similar feelings of joy. If I did not have soccer and performance training during this rock bottom time in my life, I would have gone deeper into my depression with nothing meaningful to work toward. **Purpose is crucial – to give female athletes something so impactful to them that it steers them toward a path of empowerment.** To stay focused in the face of adversity. To maintain tenacity when doubt creeps in. To hold true to a purpose when all confidence is lost. To find meaning when uncertainty hovers. To go into tackles without the fear of getting pushed down. To outrun an opponent when mental fatigue kicks in. To stay calm and keep composure during duress.

Beyond wins, losses, championships, and accolades, sports have a deeper meaning beneath the surface. It is easy to get trapped on the conveyor belt of producing, scoring, winning, and being analyzed as a statistic at the elite level. It is easy to forget who you are in this organized system that thrives on wins, losses, rankings, evaluation sheets, egos and power. It is easy to lose sight of why you play the beautiful game in the first place. It is easy to lose sight of purpose.

I challenge all female athletes to believe in their purpose, and give themselves a pat on the back for how far they've come. One of my favorite quotes by Marcus Aurelius that speaks to this topic: "Remind yourself what you have been through and what you have had the strength to endure." Purpose gives us strength to endure a lifetime of ups and downs.

Gem #2: Relationships

As a teenager, hanging out with friends who were also serious about school and sports uplifted me to be the same. While I was a soccer star in high school, I also was a straight A student, and band nerd who was first chair clarinet all four years. However, I did not excel in these on my own. I immersed myself in a variety of friend groups – athletes, band kids, and theatre kids – who also wanted to master their crafts. These were the outcasts and not the "popular" kids, but being around such inspiring and creative energy pushed me to be a more well-rounded young woman. In high school, I never hung out with the "popular" crowd who partied on the weekends while their parents were out of town. I did not drink all through high school and prided myself for not succumbing to peer pressure. I am grateful for choosing my friends wisely because I realized I truly am the average of the five people I spent the most time with.

Who a young female athlete hangs out with matters, and relationships will make or break how she shows up in the world and who she becomes as an athlete and human. She needs to get clear if her squad is elevating her to the next level and inspiring her to be a healthier person. Is her friend group always drinking alcohol, or are they nourishing their bodies? Is her friend group sedentary and staring at screens, or are they active and getting outside? Is her friend group not studying, or are they getting together for study groups?

Gem #3: Nutrition

As young a soccer player, the fast-food drive through was our go-to during tournaments. Though it was a quick option when we were on a time crunch, it was not ideal because it left me feeling bogged down in between games. I used to order cookies n' cream milkshakes, chicken nuggets, and French fries only to feel like a giant, greasy blob who was exhausted. Eventually, I shifted my nutrition by consuming things that energized me and made me feel light, rather than weighed down. I opted for things like wraps, sandwiches, and salads infused with protein and vegetables. Not only did my energy elevate, but so did my playing. Beyond my performance on the field, I felt more confident in my body when I was at school and felt like a vibrant, healthy young woman.

Gem #4: Physical Health

This one has been the nucleus of this book. Being in elite physical health is more than improved speed, improved agility, and injury resiliency. As the body ages, muscle mass, bone density, coordination, stability, and cognitive function can decline. With continued focus on physical health, female athletes can still succeed at the sport of life – to not fall when they live alone, to not suffer memory loss, to not stop enjoying leisure activities. I love sport performance and the science of exercise physiology and biomechanics, but I am the most fascinated with how all of this continues, and must be more amplified, as the female athlete rounds out her sports career.

Gem #5: Mental Health

Many believe self-care is about massages, pedicures, and escaping to a yoga retreat in the mountains. All they must do is escape, be alone, and treat themselves with peace and quiet, then poof! The self-care box is checked, and mental health is magically better, right? Unfortunately, adding luxury masks the negativity that is still in your life. You can get the deepest massage with beautiful rainfall music playing in the background, but as soon as you leave, you still go back to your toxic friends. You can go to that yoga retreat and be surrounded by peaceful souls and luscious nature, but as soon as you get home, you still go back to the stress of school.

These are quick fixes that everyone needs to be weary of, and ensure they are consistently working on their mental health. It is far more than self-care indulgences and opulent things. Instead of adding luxury, how about deleting negativity? Pure self-care is more about soothing one's internal state by doing these daily things:

➢ **Not consuming fear from television and pop culture**
➢ **Staying away from negative friends**
➢ **Not getting involved in drama and gossip**
➢ **Ending negative self-talk**
➢ **Ignoring bullies and haters**

Female athletes need to see themselves as so valuable that they do not make an ounce of time for the negativity.

Gem #6: Sleep

Without sleep, the other gems break down. Sleep regulates mood, motivation, energy, and creativity. If it is not of quality, relationships suffer, muscle recovery wanes, nutrition becomes fueled by sugar and cravings, leisure is no longer exciting, and it becomes a vicious cycle of poor overall health.

Gem #7: Leisure

It is possible to burn out from something you love, so time needs to be made for other novel activities. These include things where nothing is at stake – money, status, statistics, or accolades. Leisure is when one is immersed in the present moment, and oozes out joy, peace, and playfulness. It could be something as simple as skateboarding on the boardwalk with friends, while smelling the fresh saltiness of the ocean. It could be attending a comedy show, and belly laughing so hard it is painful in the most enriching way possible. It could be writing a book and sharing impact with the world to propel people to healthier.

Taking all of these gems into account, a female athlete will either serve her performance and life or hinder it. In fact, the biggest disasters for female athletes are these:

- ➢ **No resistance training**
- ➢ **Two sports in same season**
- ➢ **Icing injuries**
- ➢ **Pushing through growing pains**
- ➢ **Under-fueling**
- ➢ **Ignoring missed periods**
- ➢ **Not sleeping**
- ➢ **Being deficient in iron, Vitamin D and calcium**
- ➢ **Keeping toxic friendships**
- ➢ **Being addicted to drama and suffering**
- ➢ **Not making time for fun**

Of course, this list could go on and on, but the onus is on the girl to decide what strengthens her, or what weakens her. Performance is far greater than speed times and pounds lifted. It is the ability to handle the challenges of life.

CHAPTER 9: Preparing for the Sport Called Life

"Don't try to understand life. Live it! Don't try to understand love. Move into love. Then you will know and that knowing will come out of your experiencing."

- Osho

For my entire athletic career, I never had soccer as my identity, nor was it something I used to define my self-worth. I was never attached to the idea of playing in college, nor was I longing for a scholarship. I just trained and played because of my greater purpose. I enjoyed all of it wholeheartedly. Even when I went through a plethora of battles along the way – being in an abusive relationship, cracking my head open, and getting thirty stiches in my eyebrow, and so many more – I stuck with it because it meant something to my soul.

When female athletes say they want to be happier, or they want to be better at their sport, I find these to be empty statements. A better thing to say would be, "I am willing to go through many battles to be happy and get better." No one wants to be miserable, nor do people want to suffer, but the only constant in life is suffering. On the surface, humans are afraid of being miserable, but deep down, they are more afraid of staying where they are because it is making them miserable.

Being able to do the things everyone loves requires moments of failure, but it is these tiny moments that make these things worth pursuing.

This book will not benefit or armor female athletes unless they act. Sure, everyone might feel warm and fuzzy reading my words of motivation, but once they close this book, and go on to live their lives, what are they doing to prepare for the sport called life? Everyone might feel all positive and uplifted, like they can strut down the street like Beyonce, but what are they going to do when problems arise? After all, life is composed of highs and lows, something that everyone has in common. **What separates a courageous individual from a cowardly individual is accepting life's uncertainty with bravery.**

How is everyone prepared when adversity strikes? What are they doing when they get sick? What are they doing when they lose a job offer? What are they doing when a loved one passes? What are they doing when they begin to age? Are they continuing to take inventory and live out the fullest, most happy, most vibrant, most healthy, most nourished, most physically strong version of themselves? Life does not get easier as one goes through adulthood. It presents new challenges that girls must be equipped to handle. With that said, the mental and physical aspects of sports stay for a lifetime, while the tactical and technical are as fleeting as a cloud in the sky.

Reflecting on the Lifetime Impact of Coaching

To say I feel like a mom of hundreds of kids is an understatement. Although I'm not a parent myself, I totally understand what it is like for kids to accomplish amazing feats of strength and achieve their dreams. I totally feel the urge to jump up and down and get all giddy when they do something awesome. Shout out to all the parents out there, as I understand now. I have sent girls to Division I programs, including UNC, University of Maryland, Towson University, UNC Davidson, Rutgers, and to international teams.

Additionally, I have sent girls to Division III programs, including Johns Hopkins, MIT, and Carnegie Mellon. I have sent girls to pursue academics and become doctors, lawyers, and entrepreneurs. I have armored hundreds of girls with appropriate training to protect them from against ACL injuries. I am not going to turn this into a dissertation on my athletes' achievements, but wow, I am proud of what the girls, parents, and I have accomplished in the past ten years. Words cannot describe how joyful I get when I look back on how everyone has blossomed over time, and how I have been a huge part of setting the standard for training with my "work hard and be kind" culture.

I say "we have accomplished a lot" because this has not been my work alone. It has been a team effort of all the key players – from the support of the parents, to the kids putting in the work and staying committed, and me facilitating these shenanigans. The more years I coach, the more I realize I am a mentor and facilitator. It is my job to show kids their strengths, bring out their work ethic, and be the catalyst for them to discover their values and passions. I am not a "ra-ra" extroverted coach who screams and gets all hyped up. I have had my moments of being jovial, but overall, I am more on the reserved side, and lead-by-example side. If someone screws up, I give them the stare that pierces their souls and lights a fire under their butt to do better.

While it might appear that the past ten years have been all rainbows, butterflies, laughs and dumbbells, we have had our fair share of "oh crap!" moments, too. I have had athletes come into my office and spill their souls. I have had athletes cry and share their personal struggles. I have had athletes go through break-ups. I have had athletes fail exams. I have had athletes get rejection letters from colleges. When I listened to their stories, not only did I feel for them, I questioned myself relentlessly. There have been numerous occasions when I have analyzed my training methods, and had to re-commit to solving the puzzle of performance and injury reduction. I have re-taken certifications I already acquired. I have re-read *Sprinter's Compendium* and *Supertraining* multiple times. I have read hundreds of research studies. I must admit that I have had sleepless nights of tossing and turning, and asking myself how I could have run a session better. I am not perfect. In fact, I am far, far from it, but I truly believe the failures can be blessings in disguise, as well as learning curves on the path to mastery.

One of first athletes I worked with, Carly Wetzel is a shining example of what a massive failure can do for someone, and how any female athlete can create a positive turnaround from her struggles. The shortened version of the story: she was late in the college recruiting process and was unable to play at UNC, her dream school. The only way she could be on the team was to get into the school as a walk-on, and even with impressive SAT scores and a soaring GPA, she was rejected.

She called me after her she received her rejection letter, and many tears were shed. She questioned that her hard work was a total waste. Self-doubt crept in strongly, and she fell into a dark hole of despair for several weeks. Her back up plan was a small D3 school in Maryland – a great program with a stellar coach, but not her first pick. Fast forward into her second year at this university, she gets accepted at UNC as a transfer and makes the team as a walk-on.

Let me brag again: my female athletes have been awesome and have blown me away with what they accomplished. Yeah, the exercise physiology, training methods, peer-reviewed science, periodization, evaluations and data, growth and maturation considerations, performance re-assessments, speed development, are cool and essential, but nothing beats the laughs, the smiles, and the memories we have had during training. Despite some failures along the way, everyone came out on the other end with greater strength and confidence, and for that, I am incredibly proud.

I'll be honest: I do not feel successful because of where my older athletes are playing now. **I feel successful because I instilled in them a love for movement and a lifetime of taking care of their health.** Some of the best memories I have had over the years:

➢ Capture the Flag against the parents

➢ Taking ginger shots in the gym

➢ Boys' soccer vs. boys' lacrosse dodgeball as an off-season de-load week

➢ Farmer's Walk marathons and hand calluses coming in strong

- Sessions in the park and using the tree as equipment
- Heavy deadlifts
- Small-sided soccer with a large blow-up ball
- Fitness board game (the girls made this up themselves!)

It is hard to fathom how this all began with one athlete and evolved into such an inspiring community of girls who never knew each other before, but many of them now are best friends. This has been one of the highlights of my coaching career: to see a group of strangers come together to train, strive to be better, and motivate one another.

One thing I always preach to my athletes is to never get too comfortable, and the moment they feel flat is the moment they need to seek out a new challenge and change their environment. Whether this is from exposing the body to a new stimulus in the gym, or pushing their threshold during a conditioning run, or switching to a higher-level team with a new coach, the body and mind both need discomfort in order to grow. Tiny, incremental action steps toward a goal are the only path to moving forward, and the more girls are prepared for worst case scenario with the strength of their bodies and minds, everything falls into place.

To succeed in the sport called life, female athletes need to be prepared, not scared. They need to be prepared in their nutrition, sleep, and training, as well as clear on their purpose. They need to have relationships to support their dreams, and leisure to live a life that invigorates their souls. They need to take care of their mental health, manage stress, and regulate their emotions, so when something bad happens, when they screw up, or when they don't get their way, they keep churning it out. They are equipped with all the tools to be their strongest, most healthy, most resilient, most confident selves for a lifetime. **Sports do not teach life lessons, unless athletes execute them day in and day out. Sports are only a temporary moment in time, whereas life is the ultimate competition with oneself.**

CHAPTER 10: Overtime

"I will not say, do not weep, for not all tears are an evil."

– Tolkien

This book has been bittersweet for me to write, and as I typed up the last chapter, I teared up. These were not sad tears, but rather, joyful tears. I wrote this body of work with an immense amount of passion bursting from my soul, and I genuinely hope coaches, parents, and female athletes find it helpful. I wrote it from the depths of my heart, hoping to inspire girls, their coaches, and their parents to act in all areas of their performance, and not just do it for the scholarship, the improved speed times, or the bigger weight room numbers.

Admittedly, I feel I am not needed as a performance coach for young girls, because the tools outlined in this book are incredibly simple and easy to ingrain in one's life. I have no intention of continuing to coach my athletes forever. I am meant to prepare girls to go into the wild and brave the world with courage and dignity. I am meant to dig up their greater purpose and guide them toward a life of autonomy and confidence. I am meant to show them their body's strengthening capabilities. I am meant to show them that stress, sickness, and adversity should not bring them down. I am meant to show them how powerful they truly are.

After writing hundreds of blogs on youth female athletes on my website and for other publications, little did I know how powerful the written word was for young girls. Truthfully, I was compelled to write this book because I was frustrated with the youth sports system and how it is preying on female athlete insecurities and pushing them into more overtraining and injuries. I am frustrated that people roll their eyes at the basics. I am frustrated that mental and physical health are not priorities. I am frustrated at a devolving human species. I am frustrated at people not paying attention to the needs of the youth female athlete. I am frustrated girls' confidence is being destroyed. I wrote this to provide inspiration and a call for action at everyone's fingertips. I wrote this book because it will be here to refer to for a sparkle of light. I hope everyone finds it useful. **I hope everyone does not just read the information from this book, but truly makes a transformation.**

The final chapter is my blog *Soccer Saved My Life* that has been my most heavy and life changing work yet. I have gotten messages from parents and hundreds of girls saying this piece has inspired them to crawl out of depression, leave abusive relationships, fix their crippling anxiety, and overcome their insecurities. In this emotional article, girls might cry and they might think deeply, but one thing is for sure: they will feel confident to take back their power once again.

The Final Essay: Soccer Saved My Life

On my 18th birthday, I scored the winning goal in double overtime of the Maryland High School Soccer State Championship. I just capped off a perfect senior year, with an 18-0 record. It was a moment of pure joy, pride, and accomplishment.

I wasn't always this elated during my high school years, however. Before this dazzling moment, there was a tremendous amount of darkness. Just one week before this championship game, I ended an emotionally and physically abusive relationship, and was forced to pick up the shattered pieces of my heart. I was forced to jolt my mind back to reality and out of manipulation. I was forced to rekindle my self-worth and confidence. During this period of abuse, there were days I felt like I was climbing up a mountain in a mudslide; everything was so heavy and thick that I pondered if it was even feasible to plow through. There were days when I felt like there was a cold knife inside my chest, stabbing at my lungs and preventing me to breathe with ease. There were days when I felt like I was in a constant state of panic and feeling on edge about my future. There were days when I felt my gut punched and crippled by anxiety. There were days when my appetite was squashed, and I refused to eat and nourish my body. There were days when my mind was brainwashed, preventing me from realizing my own identity.

Meanwhile, on the soccer field…

There were days when I felt like I was climbing up this mudslide with perseverance. There were days when I felt like the knife stabbing my chest was just an illusion. There were days when I felt like even though my gut was punched, I was strong enough to survive. There were days when I felt like my mind was immersed in the present moment, and I was my resilient self again. There were days when the abusive words didn't take hold of me. There were days when the bruises on my arms faded. There were days when I was numb to the violence. **There were days when soccer truly saved my life.**

Even though I was going through the extremes of emotional and physical abuse, soccer always brought me back to equilibrium within my being. When I played the beautiful game, I never felt judged, berated, or criticized. I never had to endure cold words and painful punches. Rather, I felt empowered, supported, and uplifted. I felt like my true, liberated self – tuning into the present moment, the power of creativity, and the empowerment of moving my body in a healthy way. I never felt trapped, nor did I ever feel controlled.

Even after days when I was punched in the face, almost choked to death, and called the most degrading names a woman can be called, I stepped onto the soccer field in my power, in the present moment, and with confidence in myself. The heartache, the brainwash, the abuse all vanished, like a distant nightmare. To that end, soccer always reminded me of who I was in that moment. It affirmed that I was a confident and strong woman. **I am thankful because soccer propelled me out of a relationship that could've ended my life.**

Of course, my family, friends, and my therapist were an incredible support system during this time. They noticed the bruises on my body and stepped in quick. My parents called the police countless times. They also hired a psychotherapist. My dad got his lawyer involved. My best girlfriends pushed me to hang out with them. My parents were hard on me not to quit soccer. Abuse is hard for many to understand, but even after some of these measures, it was too late to heal my brainwashed psyche.

Soccer saved my life.

It was the only thing that motivated me to get out of bed during my depression. I had exciting, adrenaline-filled games to play. I had a loving team. I had a fun job to do. I had a capable body to train. I had my friendships.

You probably wonder why I'm sharing such an emotionally heavy story.

First, it's healing for me. Secondly, it's why I take my job as a youth female athlete performance coach so seriously. I want to inspire girls to love movement and their sport so much that they use both as a meaningful escape, because what's the alternative?

Toxic relationships? Harmful environments? Coping mechanisms? Partying? Trouble? Isolation? Depression?

I never felt like training and my sport were obligations. I played soccer out of pure joy, loved the game, and enjoyed movement. I trained because of my passion to get better and see how far I could raise my performance ceiling. The abuse I went through could've led me down a dark path of dramatic and inauthentic relationships, destructive coping mechanisms, and substance abuse. Fortunately, I landed on my feet and beat the opposition.

Soccer saved my life.

For this reason, I preach so loudly that young girls have a genuine love for working out, becoming better, and playing their sport. This was the reason why I wrote with such fiery, life-pondering prose, and why I published this book. I want female athletes to wake up motivated to play, to want to move, to want to do something empowering. I want them to immerse themselves in the present moment, to create without worrying about being perfect, to try a 1v1 move without judgement, to overcome challenges in the gym, to be healthy in their minds and bodies, to focus on healing their traumas, and to find fulfillment during the darkest times.

Soccer and exercise did all of this for me.

I have my parents to thank for allowing me to choose this passion without pressure or obligation. They never told me to "play better!" or "score more goals!" or "get a scholarship!" They never pushed me into soccer too early. They saved my life, too, because **they allowed me freedom to fall in love with the game with autonomy**. Autonomy surely has its way of oozing feelings of empowerment and strength during life-altering events.

Even during my lowest point, I had the courage to act and get myself out of danger. The night before my application was due for Johns Hopkins University, I remember walking down into my kitchen at midnight, and my parents still awake. A glimmer of hope birthed out of my soul as I told my mom and dad, "I just broke up with him, and I also just committed to play soccer at Johns Hopkins University." My parents cried. **At the last minute, I made the early decision application** deadline to play soccer at one of the most prestigious schools in the world.

Weeks before this life-changing decision, my parents thought I was going to quit soccer, run away with my boyfriend, and fall into a deeper depression. I came close. This last-minute decision and ounce of strength changed my life forever. It's because of this tiny moment I do what I do today.

My therapist at the time was also the catalyst for me exiting this destructive relationship, and I owe it to her for helping me crawl out when I was at my weakest. In one of our final sessions together, she handed me an article titled "10 Signs You're in an Abusive Relationship." I read it intently. I highlighted the main points and wrote notes on the pages. After diving deep in the article, I continued to research the psychology of abusive relationships. As I browsed the internet, I discovered the concept of Stockholm Syndrome and was totally jarred. I read the definition out loud: "**an emotional response that happens to abuse and hostage victims when they have positive feelings toward an abuser or captor.**" My jaw dropped. I was so floored a chill jolted up my spine and I said to myself, "this is me."

This was the moment I recognized I was willingly playing the victim. Though what my boyfriend did to me was horrific, I was the one who was incredibly manipulated, which is why I remained in the relationship for so long. I chose to be a victim, and while it was hard to admit to myself that I was also the problem, it needed to be done so I could make a change and get out fast. Coming to this realization gave me the power to step out of victimhood and claim my life back – to continue to do things that brought me joy, to surround myself with those who lifted me up, to be clear on my boundaries, and to live out my purpose.

A month after I ended this relationship, my healing process began. I started with writing about my experience. The written word has always been cathartic for me because it helps me to navigate my emotions and articulate my feelings with clarity. Ate age 18, I started writing my first book at the local library. It was a story about a straight A student, All-American youth female athlete surviving domestic violence. As I scribbled down words in my notebook, an old man in his 70s approached me.

"What are you doing?" he asked. His eyes looked like they were piercing through my soul, like he knew I was writing something heavy. In fact, I could feel he knew exactly what I was writing about and sought me out for a reason.

"I'm writing about a girl who survived abuse," I replied. Mind you, I didn't tell him it was my personal story I was writing, but I could also feel he knew.

He continued, "you know, I actually knew a girl who just suffered the same. She ended up taking her life. Keep writing." Without saying anything more, the man walked away into the book stacks.

His words "keep writing" stuck with me for a lifetime. I truly believe we crossed paths that day so he could give me a call-to-action to take a more positive route than the girl he knew who passed away. He came into my life to urge me to follow something meaningful. His presence was the glimpse of hope I needed.

Since this time, I have never returned to an abusive relationship, even though most women who experience domestic violence always do. I never got sucked back into depression. I am a rare success story and I want to inspire other young girls to see themselves as so valuable they do not have time for anything that hinders their physical, mental, emotional, and spiritual health. I want young girls to realize they control their destiny with every tiny decision they make. **Female athletes choose whether they are victims or victors. They can blame and complain, or they can take personal responsibility and live a life of purpose.** Soccer and training saved my life, and my hope after you close this book is your sport and training will save yours, too.

The strong female athlete is a force to be reckoned with, and she is waiting to bolt out of her cage.

NOTES

Chapter 2

1. Lloyd, Rhodri & Cronin, John & Faigenbaum, Avery & Haff, Guy & Howard, Rick & Kraemer, William & Micheli, Lyle & Myer, Gregory & Oliver, Jon. (2016). The National Strength And Conditioning Association Position Statement On Long-Term Athletic Development. Journal of Strength and Conditioning Research. 30. 1. 10.1519/JSC.0000000000001387.

2. 8. Brown, S. (2009). Chapter 4. In *Play* (pp. 88–89).

3. 7. Pellis SM, Pellis VC, Bell HC. The function of play in the development of the social brain. Am J Play. 2010;2:278–296

4. Jayanthi, N. , LaBella, C. , Fischer, D. , Pasulka, J. , Dugas, L. & (2015). American Journal of Sports Medicine, 43 (4), 794-801. doi: 10.1177/0363546514567298.

5. Bahr R. Demise of the fittest: Are we destroying our biggest talents? Br J Sport Med 48: 1265–1267, 2014.

6. Moesch, K, Elbe, AM, Hauge, ML, and Wikman, JM. Late specialization: The key to success in centimeters, grams, or seconds (cgs) sports. Scand J Med Sci Sports 21: e282–e290, 2011

7. Bridge, MW and Toms, MR. The specialising or sampling debate: A retrospective analysis of adolescent sports participation in the UK. J Sports Sci 31: 87–96, 2013

8. Ratey, J. J., & Hagerman, E. (2008). *Spark: The revolutionary new science of exercise and the brain (pp. 37-38).*

Chapter 3

1. Nicholas A. Beck, J. Todd R. Lawrence, James D. Nordin, Terese A. DeFor, Marc Tompkins Pediatrics Mar 2017, 139 (3) e20161877; DOI: 10.1542/peds.2016-1877

2. https://www.usyouthsoccer.org/news/acl_injury_and_the_female_soccer_player/

3. Meyer EG, Villwock MR, Haut RC. Osteochondral microdamage from valgus bending of the human knee. Clin Biomech (Bristol, Avon) 2009;24:577–582.

4. Larwa J, Stoy C, Chafetz RS, Boniello M, Franklin C. Stiff Landings, Core Stability, and Dynamic Knee Valgus: A Systematic Review on Documented Anterior Cruciate Ligament Ruptures in Male and Female Athletes. *International Journal of Environmental Research and Public Health.* 2021; 18(7):3826. https://doi.org/10.3390/ijerph18073826

5. Swanik CB, Covassin T, Stearne DJ, Schatz P. The Relationship between Neurocognitive Function and Noncontact Anterior Cruciate Ligament Injuries. *The American Journal of Sports Medicine.* 2007;35(6).943-948. doi:10.1177/0363546507299532

6. Swanik CB. Brains and Sprains: The Brain's Role in Noncontact Anterior Cruciate Ligament Injuries. *J Athl Train.* 2015;50(10):1100-1102. doi:10.4085/1062-6050-50.10.08

7. Smith, Helen C et al. "Risk factors for anterior cruciate ligament injury: a review of the literature-part 2: hormonal, genetic, cognitive function, previous injury, and extrinsic risk factors." *Sports health* vol. 4,2 (2012): 155-61. doi:10.1177/1941738111428282

Chapter 4

1. Roemmich JN, Rogol AD. Physiology of growth and development: Its relationship to performance in the young athlete. Clin Sports Med 1995;14:483

2. Piaget J, Inhelder B. The Psychology of the Child. New York: Basic Books, 1969.

3. 7. Bruinvels, G., Goldsmith, E., Blagrove, R., Simpkin, A., Lewis, N., Morton, K., ... Pedlar, C. (2021). Prevalence and frequency of menstrual cycle symptoms are associated with availability to train and compete: A study of 6812 exercising women recruited using the strava exercise app. *British Journal of Sports Medicine, 55*(8), 438–443.

4. Brown, N., Knight, C. J., & Forrest, L. J. (2021). Elite female athletes' experiences and perceptions of the menstrual cycle on training and sport performance. *Scandinavian Journal of Medicine & Science in Sports, 31*(1), 52-69.

5. Hooper, L. V., Littman, D. R., & Macpherson, A. J. (2012). Interactions between the microbiota and the immune system. *Science, 336,* 1268–1273.

6. Rankin, A., O'Donavon, C., Madigan, S. M., O'Sullivan, O., & Cotter, P. D. (2017). 'Microbes in sport' – The potential role of the gut microbiota in athlete health and performance. *British Journal of Sports Medicine, 51,* 698–699.

7. Pallavi LC, D Souza UJ, Shivaprakash G. Assessment of Musculoskeletal Strength and Levels of Fatigue during Different Phases of Menstrual Cycle in Young Adults. J Clin Diagn Res. 2017 Feb;11(2):CC11-CC13. doi: 10.7860/JCDR/2017/24316.9408. Epub 2017 Feb 1. PMID: 28384857; PMCID: PMC5376807.

8. Julian R, Hecksteden A, Fullagar HH, Meyer T. The effects of menstrual cycle phase on physical performance in female soccer players. PLoS One. 2017 Mar 13;12(3):e0173951. doi: 10.1371/journal.pone.0173951. PMID: 28288203; PMCID: PMC5348024.

9. Tremback-Ball, Amy PT, PhD; Fulton, Kaitlin DPT; Giampietro, Nicole DPT; Gibbons, Megan DPT; Kneller, Arielle DPT; Zelinka, Hayley DPT Effect of the Menstrual Cycle on Athletic Performance in NCAA Division III Collegiate Athletes, Journal of Women's Health Physical Therapy: January/March 2021 - Volume 45 - Issue 1 - p 20-26 doi: 10.1097/JWH.0000000000000188

Chapter 5

1. National Collegiate Athletic Association. *Estimated probability of competing in athletics beyond the high school interscholastic level. Available at: www.ncaa.org/sites/default/files/Probability-of-going-pro-methodology_Update2013.pdf. Accessed December 15, 2015*

2. Malina RM Early sport specialization: roots, effectiveness, risks. *Curr Sports Med Rep.* 2010;9(6):364–371pmid:21068571

3. Faigenbaum A. D., Lloyd R. S., MacDonald J., Myer G. D. (2016). Citius, Altius, Fortius: beneficial effects of resistance training for young athletes. Br. J. Sports Med. 50, 3–7. 10.1136/bjsports-2015-094621

4. Zazulak BT, Hewett TE, Reeves NP, Goldberg B, Cholewicki J. Deficits in Neuromuscular Control of the Trunk Predict Knee Injury Risk: Prospective Biomechanical-Epidemiologic Study. The American Journal of Sports Medicine. 2007;35(7):1123-1130. doi:10.1177/0363546507301585

5. Duncan, RL; CH Turner (November 1995). "Mechanotransduction and the functional response of bone to mechanical strain". Calcified Tissue International. **57** (5): 344–358. *doi:10.1007/bf00302070. PMID 8564797. S2CID 8548195.*

6. Weyand PG, Sternlight DB, Bellizzi MJ, Wright S. Faster top running speeds are achieved with greater ground forces not more rapid leg movements. J Appl Physiol (1985). 2000 Nov;89(5):1991-9. doi: 10.1152/jappl.2000.89.5.1991. PMID: 11053354.

7. Macadam, Paul & Cronin, John & Uthoff, Aaron & Johnston, Michael & Knicker, Axel. (2018). The role of arm mechanics during sprint-running: a review of the literature and practical applications. Strength and Conditioning Journal. 40. 1. 10.1519/SSC.0000000000000391.

8. Vescovi, Jason. (2013). Motion Characteristics of Youth Women Soccer Matches: Female Athletes in Motion (FAiM) Study. International journal of sports medicine. 35. 10.1055/s-0033-1345134.

9. Mathisen, Gunnar & Pettersen, Svein. (2015). The Effect of Speed Training on Sprint and Agility Performance in 15-Year-Old Female Soccer Players. LASE Journal of Sport Science. 6. 61-70. 10.1515/ljss-2016-0006.

10. Jones, P. A., Thomas, C., Dos'Santos, T., McMahon, J. J., & Graham-Smith, P. (2017). The Role of Eccentric Strength in 180° Turns in Female Soccer Players. *Sports (Basel, Switzerland)*, 5(2), 42. https://doi.org/10.3390/sports5020042

11. Spiteri T., Newton R.U., Binetti M., Hart N.H., Sheppard J.M., Nimphius S. Mechanical determinants of faster change of direction and agility performance in elite female basketball athletes. J. Strength Cond. Res. 2015;29:2205–2214. doi: 10.1519/JSC.0000000000000876.

12. Vassilis S, Yiannis M, Athanasios M, Dimitrios M, Ioannis G, Thomas M. Effect of a 4-week detraining period followed by a 4-week strength program on isokinetic strength in elite youth

soccer players. *J Exerc Rehabil.* 2019;15(1):67-73. Published 2019 Feb 25. doi:10.12965/jer.1836538.269

13. Araujo S, Cohen D, Hayes L. Six weeks of core stability training improves landing kinetics among female capoeira athletes: a pilot study. *J Hum Kinet.* 2015;45:27-37. Published 2015 Apr 7. doi:10.1515/hukin-2015-0004

14. Akuthota V, Ferreiro A, Moore T, Fredericson M. Core stability exercise principles. Curr Sport Med Report. 2008;7:39–44

Chapter 6

1. Antoneta Granic, Karen Davies, Carol Jagger, Richard M. Dodds, Thomas B L Kirkwood, Avan A Sayer, Initial level and rate of change in grip strength predict all-cause mortality in very old adults, *Age and Ageing*, Volume 46, Issue 6, November 2017, Pages 970–976, https://doi.org/10.1093/ageing/afx087

2. Panagoulis, Charalampos[1]; Chatzinikolaou, Athanasios[1]; Avloniti, Alexandra[1]; Leontsini, Diamanda[1]; Deli, Chariklia K.[2]; Draganidis, Dimitrios[2]; Stampoulis, Theodoros[1]; Oikonomou, Triantafyllos[2]; Papanikolaou, Konstantinos[2]; Rafailakis, Lefteris[1]; Kambas, Antonios[1]; Jamurtas, Athanasios Z.[2]; Fatouros, Ioannis G.[2] In-Season Integrative Neuromuscular Strength Training Improves Performance of Early-Adolescent Soccer Athletes, Journal of Strength and Conditioning Research: February 2020 - Volume 34 - Issue 2 - p 516-526 doi: 10.1519/JSC.0000000000002938

3. Nimphius S, McGuigan MR, Newton RU. Relationship between strength, power, speed, and change of direction performance of female softball players. J Strength Cond Res. 2010 Apr;24(4):885-95. doi: 10.1519/JSC.0b013e3181d4d41d. PMID: 20300038.

4. Dimeglio A, Canavese F. The growing spine: how spinal deformities influence the normal spine and thoracic cage growth. Eur Spine J 2012;21:64-70. 10.1007/s00586-011-1983-3

Chapter 7

1. Cottrell J, O'Connor JP. Effect of Non-Steroidal Anti-Inflammatory Drugs on Bone Healing. *Pharmaceuticals (Basel)*. 2010;3(5):1668-1693. Published 2010 May 25. doi:10.3390/ph3051668

2. Goldstein JL, Cryer B. Gastrointestinal injury associated with NSAID use: a case study and review of risk factors and preventative strategies. *Drug Healthc Patient Saf.* 2015;7:31-41. Published 2015 Jan 22. doi:10.2147/DHPS.S71976

3. https://www.youtube.com/watch?v=bcSr7hueQOo&t=2797s

4. Nestor, James. Breath: The New Science of a Lost Art. , 2020. Print.

5. J.E. Jan, R.J. Reiter, M.C. Bax, U. Ribary, R.D. Freeman, M.B. Wasdell

    1. Long-term sleep disturbances in children: a cause of neuronal loss

2. Eur. J. Paediatr. Neurol., 14 (5) (2010), pp. 380-390

6. Gupta L, Morgan K, Gilchrist S. Does elite sport degrade sleep quality? A systematic review. *Sports Med.* 2017; 47:1317–33.

7. Milewski MD, Skaggs DL, Bishop GA, et al. Chronic lack of sleep is associated with increased sports injuries in adolescent athletes. *J. Pediatr. Orthop.* 2014; 34:129–33.

8. Gross CR, Kreitzer MJ, Reilly-Spong M, Wall M, Winbush NY, Patterson R, Mahowald M, Cramer-Bornemann M. Mindfulness-based stress reduction versus pharmacotherapy for chronic primary insomnia: a randomized controlled clinical trial. Explore (NY). 2011 Mar-Apr;7(2):76-87. doi: 10.1016/j.explore.2010.12.003. PMID: 21397868; PMCID: PMC3077056.

9. Pattanashetty, R., Sathiamma, S., Talakkad, S. *et al.* Practitioners of vipassana meditation exhibit enhanced slow wave sleep and REM sleep states across different age groups. *Sleep Biol. Rhythms* **8**, 34–41 (2010). https://doi.org/10.1111/j.1479-8425.2009.00416.x

10. Vitale KC, Owens R, Hopkins SR, Malhotra A. Sleep Hygiene for Optimizing Recovery in Athletes: Review and Recommendations. *Int J Sports Med.* 2019;40(8):535-543. doi:10.1055/a-0905-3103

11. Telzer EH, Goldenberg D, Fuligni AJ, Lieberman MD, Gálvan A. Sleep variability in adolescence is associated with altered brain development. Dev Cogn Neurosci. 2015 Aug;14:16-22.

doi: 10.1016/j.dcn.2015.05.007. Epub 2015 May 28. PMID: 26093368; PMCID: PMC4536158.

12. Gross CR, Kreitzer MJ, Reilly-Spong M, Wall M, Winbush NY, Patterson R, Mahowald M, Cramer-Bornemann M. Mindfulness-based stress reduction versus pharmacotherapy for chronic primary insomnia: a randomized controlled clinical trial. Explore (NY). 2011 Mar-Apr;7(2):76-87. doi: 10.1016/j.explore.2010.12.003. PMID: 21397868; PMCID: PMC3077056.

13. Olafsdottir G, Cloke P, Schulz A, et al. Health Benefits of Walking in Nature: A Randomized Controlled Study Under Conditions of Real-Life Stress. Environment and Behavior. 2020;52(3):248-274. doi:10.1177/0013916518800798

14. Juyoung Lee, Yuko Tsunetsugu, Norimasa Takayama, Bum-Jin Park, Qing Li, Chorong Song, Misako Komatsu, Harumi Ikei, Liisa Tyrväinen, Takahide Kagawa, Yoshifumi Miyazaki, "Influence of Forest Therapy on Cardiovascular Relaxation in Young Adults", *Evidence-Based Complementary and Alternative Medicine*, vol. 2014, Article ID 834360, 7 pages, 2014. https://doi.org/10.1155/2014/834360

15. Bourre JM. Effets des nutriments sur les structures et les fonctions du cerveau: le point sur la diététique du cerveau [The role of nutritional factors on the structure and function of the brain: an update on dietary requirements]. Rev Neurol (Paris). 2004 Sep;160(8-9):767-92. French. doi: 10.1016/s0035-3787(04)71032-2. PMID: 15454864.

16. Mailhot G, White JH. Vitamin D and Immunity in Infants and Children. *Nutrients*. 2020;12(5):1233. Published 2020 Apr 27. doi:10.3390/nu12051233

17. Simic L, Sarabon N, Markovic G. Does pre-exercise static stretching inhibit maximal muscular performance? A meta-analytical review. Scand J Med Sci Sports. 2013 Mar;23(2):131-48. doi: 10.1111/j.1600-0838.2012.01444.x. Epub 2012 Feb 8. PMID: 22316148.

18. Hart L. Effect of stretching on sport injury risk: a review. Clin J Sport Med. 2005 Mar;15(2):113. doi: 10.1097/01.jsm.0000151869.98555.67. PMID: 15782063.

19. Harvey RH, Peper E, Mason L, Joy M. Effect of Posture Feedback Training on Health. Appl Psychophysiol Biofeedback. 2020 Jun;45(2):59-65. doi: 10.1007/s10484-020-09457-0. PMID: 32232605.

20. Weineck F, Schultchen D, Hauke G, Messner M, Pollatos O (2020) Using bodily postures to reduce anxiety and improve interoception: A comparison between powerful and neutral poses. PLOS ONE 15(12): e0242578. https://doi.org/10.1371/journal.pone.0242578

21. Nair S, Sagar M, Sollers J 3rd, Consedine N, Broadbent E. Do slumped and upright postures affect stress responses? A randomized trial. Health Psychol. 2015 Jun;34(6):632-41. doi: 10.1037/hea0000146. Epub 2014 Sep 15. PMID: 25222091.

Manufactured by Amazon.ca
Bolton, ON